JOAN CAMPBELL and her husband, Hugh, now live at Stoneybraes, just up the hill from The Sheiling, the B&B business they ran for 40 years. Her novel, *The Land Beyond The Green Fields*, was published in 2007, followed by her first book on the joys of running a highland B&B, *Heads on Pillows*, published in 2009. Her son Neil with his partner, Katrina, and their children, Shane and Fallon, continue to live close by. In 2011, Joan was awarded an MBE for her work in tourism. She continues working with the Federation of Small Businesses on their Regional Committee, and sits on the board of the Highlands & Islands Tourism Awards. She recently stepped down from seven years of writing the popular column, *Tourism Matters* in *The Northern Times* and has given up her work with VisitScotland to move on to working with Cats Protection, insisting that cats will be easier to herd than people. Retirement for Joan still seems a long way off!

Bye Bye B&B

More from Behind the Scenes at a Highland B&B

JOAN CAMPBELL

Luath Press Limited

EDINBURGH

www.luath.co.uk

First published 2012

ISBN: 978-1-908373-42-7

The paper used in this book is recyclable. It is made
from low chlorine pulps produced in a low energy, low emission
manner from renewable forests.

Printed and bound by
Martins the Printers, Berwick upon Tweed

Typeset in 11.5 point Sabon
by 3btype.com

Contents

Foreword

JOAN CAMPBELL KNOWS about the tourism industry in Scotland. She actually knows a great deal about the tourism industry in Scotland. She ran a successful B&B for 40 years, recently worked on designing a degree in tourism, was awarded the Scottish Silver Thistle for Outstanding Achievement, had several key roles within VisitScotland and the preceding Area Tourist Boards, wrote a monthly tourism column for the Scottish Provincial Press and has already written several books.

What then has she decided is the key factor in her success: the answer is both simple and complex – it's always about people.

Whether it's hosting a dinner for her favourite guests (the Gunnyeon family whose children she has watched over the years grow into adulthood and their own marriages), dealing with the many (oh, so many) idiosyncrasies' of some guests or firing the enthusiasm of other tourism enterprises for embracing quality – Joan shows us that the tourism industry is always about people.

Well, *almost* always about people – her husband ('Himself'), son Neil, his partner (and 'daughter to borrow') Katrina and her grandson and grand-daughter aren't the only characters Joan invites us to get to know in this book: the marvellously named 'Hobbit' the cat, 'Pooh' (another cat), 'Smudge' (again, a cat – but in mitigation one who thinks they are a dog), the aptly named 'Bronco' the horse (who likes Tennant's Special – sometimes *too* much), a succession of house rabbits and a flock of lambs are all vividly painted in against a backdrop of Scotland's stunning scenery.

Tourism is one of Scotland's most successful industries, providing over £4 billion Gross Value Added to the Scottish economy every year, with high levels of visitor satisfaction. The tourism related sector employs around 200,000 people in Scotland in 15,000 diverse businesses and many fragile communities are dependent upon the revenues generated by the visitor economy.

Scotland is competing against the rest of the world, in a global industry which is expected to grow from 1 billion international arrivals in 2012 to 1.8 billion by 2030. Scotland has stunning landscapes and scenery – both rural and urban, superb food and drink, world-class culture and heritage, activities, events and festivals that are world renown and our business tourism sector is securing prestigious conventions.

We couldn't deliver these results without the hard work and dedication of the Scottish tourism industry and they have the on-going support of the Scottish Government to ensure that we are in the best shape to make the most of the major opportunities that are coming our way over the next few years. The key to success in tourism is placing the individual customer's wish for a high quality, value for money and memorable experience at the heart of everything we do and ensuring it's delivered by people who are not just skilled, but passionate about what they do.

As Joan reminds us here, so vividly and with such humour and grace under pressure, it's *always* about people.

Fergus Ewing MSP
Minister for Energy, Enterprise and Tourism

Introduction

IN A REFLECTIVE MOOD, some years down the line from waving goodbye to the last paying guests who took their reluctant leave of the bed and breakfast I had run for the last 40 years, I had to have a bit of a think about my own attitude.

For the past few years I have been questioned with relentless regularity, 'Do you miss your B&B?' Now, if I answer, 'Like a hole in the head,' it would be much closer to the truth than, 'I don't know how I'm surviving it,' but what would that imply? That I did it only for the money? That it was a drag? That the visitors to our country I sheltered under my roof for all those years were nothing but a demanding distraction from all the important things I wanted to do? Sounds dreadful, yet within those statements, there lies a grain of truth.

Of course I did it for the money, but that was not the main reason. And, boy, there sure were times when it was a drag. Hot sunny days when everyone else was at the beach, there I was slaving over a stove preparing a full dinner for a multitude of different tastes. As to distraction, one had to carefully plan even a quick nip to the loo, for fear of the inevitable interruption of person, phone, doorbell, animal, child, or conscientious housekeeper muttering fiendish threats that it was all right for some, disappearing just when they were needed. There were times when there was nowhere in the house to hide. And when found, the smile had to be plastered back on. Do I miss all that?

Yet, such glitches were the antithesis of everything The Sheiling became known for. The learning curve of care allowed my reputation to grow with the years and saw me eventually leave the running of the house to employees with abilities to grow that reputation while I took off on one or other of my 'skives'. Skiving, as far as family was concerned, means leaving all the hard work to others and having a great time wandering about Scotland doing my thing then coming home exhausted due to excessive hospitality dished out by others while I am having a ball. Skiving for me is quite another story. Even the hard earned fun at times has an edge of hysteria, wondering, whether this is really happening!

But to get back to the inevitable question of whether I now miss my guests. I don't. This seems to surprise some, shock others, and only those who have been there, done it with every fibre of their being, and moved on from it, understand that to hand over your home to the enjoyment of strangers, to slowly realise that in the relentless pursuit of ensuring you are meeting all the needs of your guests, your social life becomes a thing of the past, and your priorities are forced into a reassessment that leaves family a lot further down the pecking order than their wish list dictates. In other words, doing B&B successfully, building it up into a viable business rather than supporting a certain life-style, takes over your life.

That being the case, and having only one life, a successful B&B business is more of a vocation, into which I pulled all the elements of life I enjoyed. And at the heart of that enjoyment lay the most important component of all: serving people. I had to work with people, so closing the door on the final guest could not mean I had to stop working with people. This continued in ways I would never have dreamed possible. That I should spend three of the last few years working with academics delivering skills in tourism that saw me dip the knee to royalty and have an MBE pinned on my quaking lapel was beyond belief. That I should become the Federation of Small Businesses tourism representative for Scotland, with a workload at times taking up every hour of my day, and most days of my week, while as a volunteer to the FSB cause, no pennies were added to a depleting bank balance crying out in neglect now that paying guests are a thing of the past, was surprising. That I should be roped back into boards and committees I skipped happily out of when the door closed on the guest house was beyond rational thought. Well, that's what my family hinted at. Now that I was an MBE and no longer had the direct approach of a mother who did not suffer fools gladly, statements like, 'Are you mad?' are consigned to memory. What a pity. Such direct confrontations, despite being mostly ignored, could at times make me think.

All this activity allowed me to continue on the path of working with people while we could have our home to ourselves. Himself, that man of indisputable loyalty who shared my life, was wrapped up in the joys of never having to face another scary guest, and I was wallowing in the knowledge that come the first day of April 2008, my traditional opening day of each new season, we had none to answer to but ourselves. No fevered rushing about spending a fortune to maintain expectations of both our guests and VisitScotland advisors. No nightmares of having a house full of people while every conceivable catastrophe lurked round every corner. After 40 years of such anxiety, the beckoning freedom was heady stuff.

So how come, in the ensuing years that saw us prepare The Sheiling for its inevitable sale, did I take on a workload surpassing anything to do with running a B&B? Despite being in the throes of designing and building a new home to meet our needs, our expectations, our desire to welcome friends and family and re-establish the social niceties of life that had sunk into obscurity, why was I enmeshing myself in an involvement with people again? I wasn't stupid, well, not so stupid that I didn't know the downside of what I was taking on.

There would be anxiety, angst, and trepidation in equal measure with laughter, great craic, and so much fun; life really continued much as before but at an even faster pace. The accommodation diary changed to a well-stuffed appointments diary. The small office opening off the kitchen at The Sheiling eventually changed into a spacious room at Stoneybraes, our new home just up the hill, within sight of The Sheiling and its garden. Our cats took tremendous exception to relocating to a gravel pit where the digging is hard and the mice are few.

The 'big cat', who was in actuality the smallest of the three, continued to discipline her children while letting us know her opinion of the move. Her kittens, then all of 12 years old, took to cuffing each other at every opportunity, eventually changing a warm and loving friendship into a bitter rivalry for attention that brings no change as the years roll on, not even when their mother taught us all a lesson by going into The Sheiling garden and dying there. She always did know how to grab attention.

This brings me to my last and most puzzling question of the lot. Why, after dedicating my life to working with people, am I sitting here looking at a good luck card that came with a beautiful bouquet of flowers from the Director of Quality and Standards at VisitScotland, wishing me luck in my new life working with cats?

Probably because I am determined to drag myself out of every committee, board and other involvement within tourism, but knowing how easily influenced I can be by the lure of 'if you have time would you help out with…?' I intend filling that space with work of a different calibre.

So, in an act of sabotage to any such threats to my determination to lay tourism aside, I made the sudden, and I have no doubt barmy, decision that I would offer my services to my favourite charity, Cats Protection, but not as a behind-the-desk administrator having to meet and debate and deal with people. Instead, I will be dealing with cats. I will be dealing with a different breed to some of the cats I've met in tourism, myself being only recently referred to as 'the cat among the pigeons' when thanked after some rather sticky negotiations when delivering an event in my home counties of Sutherland and Caithness.

In May of this year, at my final meeting with VisitScotland, I stood down, saying I had at last seen the light and I was tying up all my spare time to work with cats, because I had come to the inevitable conclusion that cats are much easier to herd than people.

What follows is the story of the last year in my life at The Sheiling, with all its animals and its people, much of it written as it happened, the rest reflections brought on during that eventful time. It was a special year. The frisson of excitement that came from knowing we were going into our last season at The Sheiling was tempered by the enormity of what we were actually undertaking. Closing down an established business with its established income. Would we survive financially? Would we get a buyer? And most daunting of all, would we have the new home we dreamed of fit for occupation when we did get a buyer for the guest house? Visions of being homeless did not sit well on our anxious shoulders.

Little did I know that by the time we moved towards that dream, we would hit a downturn in selling houses, a huge rise in building costs and a collapse in banking that saw investments melt and anxiety chip away at the corner stone of my optimism. Friends began to meet me with, 'It's a bad time to be selling,' rather than the familiar, 'Have you people in tonight?'

Not having second sight, I was completely unaware of the sleepless nights to come as I gleefully set about filling my rooms during that final season. There was nothing to warn that come July, I would be looking at empty beds, courtesy of BT, turning my best intentions into tantrums that would have done credit to any two year old.

It's a blessing that to compensate for that downside, we had many good times. Towards the end of the season we were able to accommodate for an entire weekend our favourite family, the Gunnyeons, as they took over the house, the children now adults with their partners, the atmosphere reminding us of the days when various couples booked in at the same time each year for dinner, bed and breakfast. The warmth and excitement of looking after such convivial people was the real reason to get involved with the precarious business of serving the holidaying public.

So why am I now pulling away from any work that involves tourism and people when I had given it a lifetime's service? My detractors say with incredulous scepticism, 'She says she's going to work with cats. Did you ever hear the likes!'

The reason to get away from tourism is easily enough explained. I see myself as being no longer qualified, no longer earning my crust from the coalface of tourism. So why should I see fit to sit on boards and committees debating the policies that affect those who are dependent upon the economies of scale that sees tourism at the forefront of Scotland's earning power? My very first argument on the very first board I sat on was, why should staff who have never run a business in their lives have so much power over owners faced with the difficulties of commercialism?

After closing The Sheiling, being employed for three years in the business of building a degree in tourism and hospitality was a great excuse to get back into the heart of all that makes tourism tick. When that contract came to its natural end in September 2011 after the degree was validated, I began the long, slow process of getting back my life.

With a desire to continue doing some voluntary work, why cats rather than people? It's not because they don't answer back, believe me. A swift scratch from an indignant cat can sting far longer than the retort of a colleague when your view is questioned. A dear friend, young enough to be my granddaughter, has as big a passion for cats as I have and we're going to go into this together. What lies ahead is an open book, but this book you are about to read is a tale of a different kind, the reality of taking paying guests into your home, the highs and the lows of that last year, tales of looking back at past debacles, getting it together with the animals and people that are woven into the complexities of a road I did not chose to travel when I was inveigled into those first tentative steps.

Would I have had it different? Not for one minute. It is what made me what I am.

'The best way to find yourself is to lose yourself in the service of others' Mahatma Gandhi 1869–1948.

I wonder if 'others' includes cats!

Joan Campbell
18 June 2012

I

Setting Myself Free

IF I DIDN'T ANSWER the phone it would go on to the answer service, I thought as I sat there idly, chin resting in both my hands, elbows propped on an incredibly tidy desk, computer pushed aside. I stared, wondering at the intensity of the ringing; a strident demand, when all else in my life was grinding to an ignominious halt. And this time, for sure, it wasn't my fault!

Languidly, with little interest in the needs of the caller I reached out a hand. Instead of my usual perky, 'The Sheiling, how may I help you?' I drawled a disinterested 'What?'

'Aaoow. Good Morning,' came the cultured sound of a woman of breeding. Straightening my back, just a little, but still not that bothered, I refrained from replying, 'Says who!' To have responded in agreement was quite beyond my present state. It wasn't a good morning. Nor had any morning, afternoon, or evening been good for weeks now. Circumstances beyond my control, I insisted to anyone who would listen, though most people were avoiding me. The few friends I had left, members of the family who put up with my capriciousness, and the cats, especially the cats, all circumnavigating to best effect.

'Can I help you?' I managed, remembering I was supposed to be a stalwart of the hospitality industry, or had been up until I breezed into the final few months of running what had been termed one of Scotland's quality B&BS. 'Aaoow,' came the disembodied voice, sounding just like one of the cats trying to convince me that their needs were greater than mine. 'Have you a free room available for the 7th and 8th of September?'

My head lifted out of my hand and with an arch of the eyebrows I moved the phone in front of my eyes to have a bit of a stare at it. What next! 'Hellaow! Are you still there? For myself and my husband. An en suite room. Free for the 7th and 8th September?'

'No! Definitely not, I do not have a free room,' I said with considerable dignity, but emphatically.

'Aaoow, it *is* the end of August and I suppose you are very busy.' I didn't bother saying no to that as well. 'Do you have a free room for the following week? We are quite flexible, you know, and we did so want to stay with you. Such a good recommendation. We would take a twin or a double, so long as it's en suite,' the voice persisted.

'No, I can't give you that,' this time tempering my tone by adding a brisk 'Sorry!'

'Aaoow! My goodness. When is your first free night, then?'

Really! First a free room. Now a free night.

'Sorry, we can't give you that.'

'You have no availability at all?"

'Oh. Yes, we have availability, tonight, as a matter of fact.' I was very positive about that.

'Yes, my dear, but I did mean after the 7th of September.' You could hear patience being stretched as the realisation dawned that she could be dealing with the monkey and not the organ grinder. Obviously, she would ask for the proprietor if this got out of hand. I always had the undisputed position of *the* Proprietor but I had not been the Organ Grinder for the last 10 years, not since the man Himself, that quiet man of resolute intentions I married when I was still a child and easily influenced, retired from his job as a Rigger on a North Sea oil rig and started to tell me how to run my business of 30 years standing, inveigling himself into the position of Top Dog whilst I scurried about, like a scalded cat; although now nobody in this household scurried about at all.

'We have availability, right through to the end of the season,' I assured, not certain whether to be happy or as deeply concerned as I should be about that fact. It was only in the last few days I had entered into this 'who cares' attitude, and isn't attitude everything in the tourism industry? You'll soon appreciate that if you stick with me. It would be nice if you did, with everyone else melting into the safety of the other side of the road. Even the cats, mice firmly gripped between dripping teeth, take a quick detour upon sight of me and the mouse is never seen again, whereas up to this latest catastrophe in my life I was given first choice of this precious gift. I had to be quick with the Pooh, a flicker of no-thank-you and it was down her throat before I could change my mind. The Hobbit, when a mouse was offered which was not often, he being a rabbiter, was much more of a gentleman and made a few prodding 'oh-surely-you-can-manage-this-little-morsel' gestures before delicately removing the carcass to some private corner to enjoy, a sanctimonious look of, 'well, I did offer,' on his handsomely striped face.

'Aow,' I was reminded by my cat-like enquirer on the other end of the line, 'Excuse me, but I understood you to say you did not have a room available on the 7th and 8th.' The voice went from puzzlement to irritability in the one sharp sentence.

'Ah, there was me thinking you were looking for a free room when all you wanted was availability. You see, we stopped giving rooms away free years ago, when word got around. Everybody, even a horse, wanted to get a free room for the night...'

'Aaoow,' she interrupted, hesitant now, not sure if she should be following this through. 'We don't have a horse, just the two of us, if that makes any difference.' We did once board a rather large horse in our stables whilst it accompanied its rider on a Land's End to John O' Groats trail. Free board often sought, was mostly given, to charity walkers, so why not a charitable horse?

The despair in my caller's voice brought me back to reality. Why was I doing this, being deliberately obtuse to this innocent woman? My only excuse was being driven mad by the boredom of having little to do, not since BT spirited away my email address, key to all my advertising and marketing material, through which I took much of my business. They took weeks to sort it out, never admitting to selling the account as I suggested, just mislaying it and sharing part-blame with Yahoo, the bad boy who did it and then ran away, leaving them with the pieces to pick up. I was in pieces, I can tell you that, after a few exchanges with the Indian call centre, and, if you want to know more about that fiasco, fast-track to Chapter 6, 'Sabotaged by British Telecom', sub-titled, 'How to make lasting relationships with the enemy whilst doubting your sanity'.

I sat up properly this time and put on my broadest smile – smiles do carry into the voice our 'how to win friends and influence people' advisors tell us – adopting my warmest, most welcoming voice, efficiency sparking off my new-found squared shoulders, I said, 'Would you like me to make a reservation in one of our nicest en suite rooms, overlooking Melvich Bay for the nights of the 7th and 8th of September?' I was convinced she would no longer want the room, and I would never have to answer for my irascibility.

'Aow, yes we would, but my dear, do tell your mother that I shall telephone back this evening to confirm the booking and have the pleasure of speaking with Mrs Campbell herself.' Many moons ago, before I became entrapped in this life of servitude, I was often taken for the daughter of the household when I was more in the mode of a young girl, with my long dark hair, swinging 60s clothes and fashionably skinny frame. But that was then, and this was now, and while the years had caught up with me, unfortunately the sense to stop taking the piss when things were heading for dire straits had not.

'Who shall I say called?' I asked in my little-girl voice, hoping if the booking came about, I could pass off Katrina, who knew a thing or two about taking the piss. I don't have a daughter, but I do have one to borrow, to love, and to treat just as my dreams had told me a daughter should be treated, in those long gone days when I believed one would appear under the gooseberry bush after delivering a fine son and thinking 'I'm not doing that again!' Happily, that fine son found Katrina, his partner of many years, delivering up to us between them, one grandson, one granddaughter and one dog, as well as a fluctuating number of fish. I'm inclined to overfeed the fish when they're left in my care, which probably accounts for the fluctuation. The whole bundle brings into our lives barrow-loads of fun and laughter, plenty to worry about as we share the bad times along with the good, Katrina as ready to dig me out of a hole as I am ready to do a bit of spade work for her, before our usual capitulation of asking Neil to dig us both out before his father cottons on to our latest disaster. Your usual family, except that Himself calls our little family, 'that tribe over the road'. What they call us, we have yet to find out. But someone will tell us. They always do, in small communities.

The cultured voice of my caller brought my thoughts back with a bump. 'Lady MacInlay. Just tell Mrs Campbell that Lady MacInlay will call back to reserve the room.' My eyes popped. Aaahh! Trust me, in the mood to wind someone up, I had to go for the top echelons of society. In this trade we like to add to our reputations by believing we can play host to the best in the land, and no amount of untoward behaviour will disavow us of the belief a title accompanies that select best! Many years ago, when I first started to shift walls instead of furniture, to meet my growing ambitions of where I wanted to be in five years time, as the business planners espouse, we had just completed a huge renovation when we played host to a Lord and his Lady. They'd been supposed to stay at Melvich Hotel in its years of catering to the undisputed toffs as they fished the salmon out of the Halladale River, and were sent courtesy of the Hotel's Manageress who had over-stretched herself in the belief she had a room more than she actually possessed. Been there, done that, so I gladly accepted the booking, not finding out I had the aristocracy on my hands until the day of arrival, when I did a double-take at their car. I didn't even have the curtains up in the new dining room! But my guests proved themselves delightful, her Ladyship sitting with me one companionable morning, discussing this that and the next as we pushed curtain hooks into heavy demanding material, eventually standing back to admire the finished results with agreeable nods of satisfaction. I bet she felt much more one of us than I one of them. I could just hear her as she slipped into the Bentley that fine morning, boasting, 'I've never had to do that before!'

And here I was, blowing the next opportunity to end my career of 40 years with yet another Lady, although, when they did actually arrive, she was accompanied by a Knight rather than a Peer of the Realm. Little did I know then I would be invited to join him in the ranks of those called by Her Majesty to be appointed a member of the Civil Division of our most Excellent Order of the British Empire. I, of course, as an Ordinary Member; a sword in the hand of Her Majesty may well have proved too tempting so close to a head that had taken the mickey out of her beloved son and heir. I speak of a newspaper article dubbed 'The Prince and the Flying Crown' another of my unfortunate experiences in life at the hand of fate, involving HRH The Prince of Wales which I had the temerity to immortalise in print. But as it happened, it was the Prince himself who endowed me with the Honour, and he and I had a bit of a giggle, prompting Katrina to demand why he had spent longer with me than with those worthy others, and why was he laughing at me. 'With, dear child, with,' I replied with an air of mystery. Such conversations, never to be repeated to ordinary members of the public, were nevertheless sufficient to put me off my quickly rehearsed stroke, after a handsome Palace lackey had put us through our paces before the presentation. Piece of cake, I thought, but such an entertaining confab was enough for me to forget my three steps backwards and the final curtsey before I skedaddled. So, that sword could still be hanging over my head!

Still, I was inordinately proud to have under my roof a man who dedicated himself to 'the cause of good and the fight against evil and injustice'. My eventual Honour did not require such a singing up to, which is as well, because had I his auspicious ear of an evening, I could have told him about plenty of goings on of injustice in the tourism industry!

My eminent guests' desire to find another place just as happily suiting them as The Sheiling, despite the downright impudent behaviour of the daughter of the house, whom they never met, gave me a small window of opportunity to cast a little teasing revenge against some of the injustices I had suffered in the past.

A colleague, in the area where the good Sir Knight and his Lady wanted to be next, had stuck her nose in the air so often at many hospitable accommodations, including my own, with so much self-satisfied disdain, I knew she would jump at the chance to boast a Sir and his Lady breakfasting under her superior care. Knowing full well she was already booked, I rang with the enquiry. Her dismay at being unable to accept this bounty, and my assurances not to be so concerned, I would get them into the house of her biggest rival, was worth all the digs and subtle insults cast in my direction before I realised that there are some people you are better off without. Such fun did not often come my way and I still smile at the memory. It doesn't take a lot to please me, despite what BT say.

And that was just the start of setting myself free from the hectic world of B&B, waving a gleeful goodbye, never realising for one minute that what I would be stepping into next put B&B in the shade when it came to demands and sleepless nights!

2

No More Bums In Beds

THE MINUTE WORD got about that this was my very last season, I was faced with genuine concern rather than the expected agreement, it was about time I took the plunge.

'What on earth will you do with yourself now?' A puzzled look on the face of a colleague showed she genuinely worried for my future. In fact, the look said, what future!

All my life I was used to getting looks, looks with a sceptical edge to them because of what I was doing, what I had done, or what I was rumoured to have done. That last was a look and a half, worst was usually reserved for what I should have done, but most were for what I was about to do. Walking the straight and narrow of other people's expectations proved well nigh impossible, as well as boringly restrictive, so I took the liberty of pleasing myself to a degree, a very small degree really. Just sufficient to raise brows and initiate the look, when you live in a small community, with a big memory.

Questions over the prospect of me having nothing to do might have been genuine concern over forthcoming hours and days, culminating in weeks and months of idleness. For surely, having reached an accumulation of years, allowing some kind of discretion, none would actually credit me with running amok. It was difficult to believe that the same people who were now concerned I would wither on the vine of having nothing to do were the very ones who had, years ago, happily informed enquirers as to my position in life, 'Oh, Joan's not doing anything now. She just does bed and breakfast!'

If you read *Heads on Pillows* you'll know my reaction to that appraisal. Suffice to say, it was not kindly. So what now? Here I am, gazing longingly into the prospect of retirement, 40 years down the line from that tentative start of luring people, like a speculative spider with an eclectic taste in flies, into my parlour. Loving it and hating it in equal measure, this job gave the impression you did little but haul in cash, cash with no outlet other than your back pocket. In effect a job more demanding than any in the hospitality industry and just as cash guzzling. So much depended upon that vital barometer to success... attitude.

'Attitude! Attitude! There's nothing wrong with *my* attitude, I can tell you.' Arms akimbo, face red as a turkey cock denied his wicked way with swift-of-foot hens, I lambasted the figure in front of me. 'It is you who has the attitude problem. I'm ab-so-lute-ly affronted! In fact, I should remove you from my doorstep forthwith. Coming here, implying my prices are a rip off! The *cheek* of it!'

With an attitude straight out of Fawlty Towers, I had waited over 30 years to give vent to unbridled outrage, stemming from the days when visitors often arrived with the domineering notion they could berate you on your own doorstep before having a clue what your hospitality, or indeed your home, had to offer. Politely, and smiling like a two-faced crocodile, you told them where to go – to find somewhere more suited to their purse – while you seethed inside. And it all boiled over into a vent for those long suppressed feelings.

Backing away from me, my would-be guest gasped, 'I never meant to offend. I just thought £170 per person for a double room, without facilities, and no breakfast, may be a wee bit excessive. Probably not though,' he added as he fled. But not back to his car, just to the corner of the room, accompanied by a round of applause. For this is not a scene from my chequered career as a B&B wifie; it became for a time, the new way of delivering encouragement to proprietors of hospitality businesses. Advising them not to revert to attitude when faced with the many contretemps that will arise, when prospective customers arrive unexpectedly on the doorstep, or the reception desk, in a belligerent frame of mind.

This was 'Pride & Passion', who counted among their friends Muriel Grey, Nick Nairn and Pete Irvine, delivering the innovative idea of amusing with short sketches to prove actions speak louder than words when lessons must be learned. Set up with the backing of the then Scottish Executive to encourage good practice within the hospitality industry, it took them a few years to hit on this novel and potent assimilation of how bad service could affect any business when proprietors, managers, staff, even the resident cat if inclined to haughtiness, cared little for the comfort and expectations of their guests. A team of actors were commissioned, at considerable cost, to set the scene, with interaction from participating trade members on how to behave badly, and how to behave impeccably, using exactly the same words in each sketch, but with different body language incorporating lots of attitude accompanying the words. We were encouraged to join in, and of course it all got too much for me and I couldn't resist a bit of an adlibbing tirade!

Apart from that indulgent display, the lesson was cleverly accomplished and proved that attitude was key to success, or disaster, dependent upon word emphasis, facial expression and body language. Not what you say but the way in which you say it!

'Pride & Passion's' inaugural performance with players was within reach, a mere 80 mile round trip to the town of Wick, a reasonable drive in comparison with some distances considered to be well within my radius. So I enticed the local college to send along students from their hospitality courses. Having a seat on the board, I had my own passion for seeing these young people make the successful transition from student to tourism industry worker.

It was a risk. They could have seen it as a glorious skive, this generation so encouraged to tell it as it is, could well have given me a black mark by saying it was a load of old rubbish. But they thought it a memorable lesson, and participated with enthusiasm, raising my expectation that some of them may well be in there for the long haul, not just a gap filler to abandon when the going got tough. We were all given T-shirts with the 'Pride & Passion' logo prominently displayed across the front. Mine lay in the car for days until one sunny morning I activated a chain of events that saw a complete reprint of all 'Pride & Passion' products.

T-shirts were never my thing but with the sun up and shining, heading towards the garage back door to pick up fruit for breakfast from 'the shed' as Connie, my one-time helpmate and friend, christened our well-stocked garage, I glanced at the pristine T-shirt abandoned on the back seat of the car.

I tried on the garment, which being white, nicely matched my jeans with its blue printed logo, 'Pride & Passion', on the front and PASS IT ON in bold capitals across the back. The man I married, Himself, now firmly ensconced in my kitchen having retired from the oil rigs some years ago, believing himself to be my Managing Director, had to keep an eye on me. Who kept that eye on me all the years I built up the business was in the remit of the village gossips until I became a boring workaholic, but since Himself threw in his lot by insisting if Connie's ill health stopped her coming back, then he, and not some scary new person, would take over. 'You actually mean, you'll replace Connie. Become a member of my staff?' I scoffed at the very thought of it.

'You know perfectly well I can't replace Connie, but when you were ill, Connie and I were a great team. I can't work with anyone else and if she's not coming back, you can have a bash at replacing Connie and I'll do all the sorting out. I'm not working with anyone else,' he warned and meant it. Not that anyone else could easily be found within the walk-to-work quiet area we lived in, and I knew he meant it. When I was off skiving, as they loved to call my dedicated volunteer work on the various boards and committees for tourism I served upon, he had become part of the mainstay of the household. It was Connie or him.

I dashed to the phone. 'Connie, are you absolutely sure that your back is killing you? Himself won't work with anyone else but you.'

'Well,' came the smiling reply – I could tell she was amused – 'that's nice to know, but I can't do it any more. So much to do at home now, and I know fine, you'll get on grand.' It was no use. It was going to be Himself or nothing, and already he had his eye on the top job – meaning we would have a solid think about doing some things at least, his way. I suddenly found myself with a boss, something I had ditched with great glee when waving goodbye to my days as a slightly whackie, but never whackie-backie, secretary. We did not require the use of artificial stimuli to conjure up ways of making our days pass very quickly, skimming the edges of never quite caring if we were secure in our positions for the following day. Such was our lack of respect for the jobs we held, they being plentiful and we, the skilled workforce, being the scarcer commodity.

So there I was, the morning of the downfall of my only venture into wearing a T-shirt, doing the job allocated, cutting up the fresh fruit for breakfast whilst the boss administered to the porridge, when that strange feeling came over me that I was being watched. A couple of furtive glances confirmed my suspicions and I caught a familiar disapproving look cast in my direction.

Eventually, compelled to turn round and face my accuser, I gave an exasperated, 'What? What is it? What have I done now?'

Sighing the sigh of the hard-put-upon, he patiently replied, 'You're not going to wear that in front of the guests, are you?'

'Wear what?' I puzzled, staring at the front of my blue jeans for signs of spillage, mud, cat fur, sticky paw marks – not the cats but the grandchild – cats being much too fastidious for that, I saw nothing out of place.

'Not the jeans. That T-shirt. I thought Katrina or Neil had left it lying in the car, and I wondered to myself, what next!' Indignation was taking a grip of him. I didn't usually get into trouble before seven in the morning. It was obviously going to be one of those days!

'It's a clean...' I managed before he cut in with, 'Is that what you would call it? Clean? Well, I don't think I would call that exactly clean. I said to myself, what next will they be wearing, that pair over the road, but not for a minute did I think *that* belonged to you,' the finger of suspicion aimed directly at my proudly displayed logo.

'That pair over the road' was our son and his partner of many interesting years, parents of our much loved grandson, approaching a precocious four and doing an overnight at the time of the T-shirt incident. Himself had been able to take his eagle eye off me to occasionally cast its gimlet gleam upon those whom he affectionately labelled 'the tribe' after Shane's arrival despite being only three in number. First it was, 'that fellow', then 'that pair', and now 'that tribe' in their newly built home on the land across the road from us. It kept him very busy but now it was I who drew the penetrating gaze of our paternal manager and he was far from being amused.

Seeing the seriousness of the look on his face, I whipped off the T-shirt just as a guest wandered into the hall and had a peek through our glass doors.

Glancing through the glass doors became part of the charm of the house since changing all the wooden fire doors for beautiful clear fire glass, decorated tastefully with engraved glass imprints causing no end of admiration and photographic opportunities, particularly from our foreign trade. We made the change in order to let in lots of light and create a friendly ambience, where guests could look into kitchen or lounge and dining-room and be happy to see all was well. On the other hand it was brilliant for glimpsing whoever was in the lounge and avoiding them if evasion were required, as happens, everyone not always being totally compatible with everyone else. Many a time we wished we came into the avoidance category, but somehow we never did, and a firm stance had to be taken or you could end up cooking the breakfast in front of an appreciative audience. They stood video-cameras in hand, beside a team of feline observers who gave vent to unwanted and very vocal criticisms with exaggerated tail flicks, as you sweated it out, plying your trade in front of the cooker. At least the cats didn't photograph the evidence of any ineptitude to take back to the States to dine out on in years to come, gently deriding the quaint ways of their Scottish hostess!

Our guest quickly averted his eyes from my semi-clad state to swing out the front door for his early morning constitutional, no doubt abashed by the antics going on in the kitchen, me in my bra and Himself standing over me with the wooden spurtle from the porridge, waving it about menacingly. Being a true Highlander, he required much use of hands, and whatever they happened to hold, to emphasise his point, and boy, did he have a point that particular morning.

I peered at the T-shirt. I had not really looked at it before, used to seeing the 'Pride & Passion' logo since its inception. I never was a particularly observant person but now I gave a gasp of understanding, and immediately added insult to injury by bursting into loud laughter.

'Listen,' I implored. 'That says 'Pride & Passion'.'

'Pride and passion, my foot! It clearly says, 'Prick & Passion'.'

'OK, I know it looks like 'Prick & Passion', but it's not, honestly. It's a new type of font.'

'Font! Font? What kind of new-fangled carry on is that? And for you to be wearing it on a T-shirt.' I could smell the porridge singeing and that was a real bad omen.

'Font's a style of type and that's the name of the company I got it from.' But I couldn't stop laughing, which did not help, until his own humour got the better of him as he dived to save the porridge, shaking his head, insisting he had never seen the likes. How could I have missed such a cracker, mind already conjuring up the good giggle I could get out of deciphering this unusual script the wrong way!

'Well, it's 'Prick & Passion' it looks like to me! And if that's not bad enough, look at the rest of it. Pass it On! Scrawled across your back. It's hardly what I would expect you to be wearing to serve breakfast on a Sunday morning.'

'What difference does Sunday make?' I remonstrated, trying to gain some ground. When you do B&B, every day is the same until you become inventive, by way of reminding yourself there are actually different days, us not being adherents to the once-a-week, Saturday night only brigade. Much more as-and-when-you-like-it performers, given the opportunity, the energy, and the time, and I'm talking about going out for a social drink in case I just may be misunderstood.

That morning, our grandson Shane had been hovering about us, as he so often did in his early years and was clamouring to know what the remonstrations were about.

'What are you saying, Gwanny? What is Papa saying?'

'Nothing,' I said as I rushed upstairs to change and consider doing what the T-shirt advocated: pass it on, to his mother, so she could have a good laugh too. Most of the usual hilarity caused by Himself comes from his degree of deafness, the subject, his interpretation, and how close to a divorce we came in the ensuing meaningful discussion! He was right though, the fancy script really did look like a *ck* and not a *de*.

By then I not only sat on many committees and boards, furthering the cause of tourism, but wrote a monthly column in one of the Scottish Provincial Press publications, *The Northern Times*. Recovering from the episode in the kitchen, later that day, I ended my column for the month in the usual fashion with a humorous piece under its standard heading of And Finally…, a condensed version of the 'Pride & Passion' fiasco. Staff from a lot of the tourism agencies read the column and I soon learned that the team behind the 'Pride & Passion' movement were just a tad put out at such optical liberties taken with their name. Before long, there was a reprint of all the material using a different font, which left no doubt as to their mission statement.

I could always rely upon Himself, whom I nicknamed Skimbleshanks after that most reliable of cats in T S Eliot's *Cat of the Railway Train*, always behind me, ready to remind me that facts were facts.

Take this very morning, for instance. Recovering from a particularly nasty cold with about three square inches of what is not a very big face anyway covered in unsightly cold sores, I at last thought I would venture forth to one of the meetings I had studiously avoided, not to protect my dear colleagues from my halo of germs but because, by comparison, a scabby cat looked a lot better than I did!

Upstairs, a few deft strokes of the trowel aided by a half-inch redundant paint brush made a reasonable job of presenting my abused face in half decent shape to the outside world. Downstairs, I said to Himself, 'How do I look now?'

He put down his coffee cup and wandered over to scrutinise. 'Like a million dollars!' Goodness me! It sounded absolutely sincere.

Heading back to his coffee, he looked back and saw a slow smile of pleasure spread over my heavily camouflaged face. 'That is… in comparison with what you looked like a few days ago.' Then he peered at me closely before adding, 'Mind you, I don't have my glasses on!'

Picking up his cup, he gave his final verdict. 'You'll do… I suppose!'

Bless him. A bit of home truth when you may just be ready to delude yourself keeps feet firmly grounded in reality! He's a realist, he insists, when I accuse him of drowning my optimism in the rough seas of his pessimism.

Then, into this world of male veracity came that other authoritative figure in my life, my grandson. Shane, in the first three years of his life, was my constant shadow and a firm believer in, 'keeping an eye on Gwanny!'

'Hey, little man,' a guest said to him as he followed me into the dining-room, that long ago morning. I was now resplendent in a pristine, logo-free white blouse; the default T-shirt consigned to the way-too-full 'wear it for a laugh' drawer. 'What you doing today, then?'

He turned to the 'gestis' as he fondly called them all, and shook his head. 'Gwanny's in deep trouble. For saying bad words. Papa says her's not to say bad words 'bout the gestis!' That was his interpretation and he was sticking to it. Raised eyebrows all round the table proved each was wondering which one had caused sufficient offence to draw my ire in the privacy of the kitchen.

Actually, the idea of the movement called 'Pride & Passion' was an exemplary one, as are many initiatives encouraging the service industry to embrace the hospitality you would expect as a natural response to the needs of who pays the piper. However, as some of us know to our cost, such needs can at times be met with an injection of proprietorial authority, enough to keep a control freak owner in Happy Pills for the duration of your stay. Why is it that bad owners or managers are either so laid back they are bone idle, or so uptight they expect to take total control of not just the air you breathe, but how and when you breathe it? Mind you, the notorious Blackpool-style notices of 'DO NOT' do this and 'DO NOT' do that which had spread into many Scottish B&Bs when grudging proprietors took up the cudgels of the 'who dare meddle with me' style landlady, are thankfully now consigned to dust bins. The notices, not the landladies, unfortunately.

The man who planted the seed of the 'Pride & Passion' movement in the fertile imaginations of some like-minded colleagues, Peter Taylor of the Town House Company, Edinburgh, worked hard to bring it all about. Peter, up until 2007, was chairman of The Scottish Tourism Forum, a large and dynamic board with the usual mix of trade representatives and agency personnel. Set up a number of years ago, it was supported by the Scottish Executive as a means through which the trade could bring their concerns to the very top of the tourism sector headed by the then Tourism Minister, Patricia Ferguson. Considering the antics of her predecessor, the fiery Lord Watson, she made not too bad a fist of it! At the time of writing, we have First Minister Alex Salmond at the head of the first Scottish Nationalist Party Parliament, recognising tourism as vital to the future of enterprise in Scotland. He had made the wise decision to shift the portfolio for tourism into the hands of Jim Mather, the Minister for Enterprise, Energy and now including Tourism. However, some people at the very top of the Tourism tree in Scotland do not agree with this change which aligns tourism with energy and enterprise instead of sports. How anyone could disagree with such a change, actually a reversal back to where tourism was from the first days of the new Scottish Parliament – hand in glove with enterprise – greatly surprised me. One thing I am sure we who work all the hours God gives us to ensure tourism is alive and kicking in Scotland, will agree on is that tourism and energy go hand in hand!

It's all very well and good, liaising with our Parliamentary representatives if you live south of the great divide between the rural Highlands and Islands of Scotland and the Central Belt. The vast majority of activities, meetings and goings-on remain firmly rooted in that busy corridor of power, leaving the rest of us, in the northern counties and I'm very firmly told, the Borders, the logistical nightmare of sitting there with little impact upon decision making. Unless we can afford the time to head south, or north, towards officialdom, hopefully taking the voice of our remote, visitor-friendly, areas with us.

Getting out into the thick of things is always good. Travel, even when harassed by the demands of agendas and schedules, fair broadens the horizons and puts you in the mode of the customer. This sure opens your eyes to what we do, and do not do, to our valuable visitors, and how many Basil Fawltys it takes to change the lightbulb – that is, if it ever gets changed!

Himself had seen a bit of the world before we settled down to married life yet our first 13 years together saw only one holiday. This came about when our son was a year old and I was persuaded to join my romantically-minded husband in a caravan, where he worked, and continued to work throughout our 'holiday', in the beautiful west coast village of Plockton. The area was stunning in its scenery, the people hospitable to a fault and he and his workmates determined to carry on as normal: work a 12 hour day and fit in a four hour drinking spree in the local pub as many nights as possible, despite this female thrust into their midst. It may sound like a lot of fun, but it wasn't and when I returned home, our child Neil, having been thoroughly spoiled by my sister Sandra and her husband Malcolm, refused to have anything to do with me!

From then on in I determined to take control of any further forays into the unknown, but it took a lot of bums in beds before I had enough of the readies to bring my travel ambitions to fruition. By then, Himself was tucked in nicely on a North Sea oil rig, adding to the goodies pile. So I let my imagination run riot before the triumphant question, 'Guess where we're going this time?' drew its shocked response as he listened to the crackling telephone line, convinced he couldn't possibly be hearing right.

It was long ago and few, certainly from our area, ventured to remote regions of Venezuela to fly in a lop-sided two-seater plane over Angel Falls, or various locations of India. On the inevitable trip to the Taj Mahal I fell in love with a camel I dated every day but Himself wiped all the lovingly taken pictures of my desert friend from the film. He was adamant it was an accident though I had my doubts. I managed to go two whole hours without speaking to him that day, which must be a bit of a record, speaking to all and sundry being essential to my survival. Now age has provided the pure magic of speaking to yourself as a way of life, with no answers needed to the constant questions you ask! The downside only begins when you start answering yourself back.

Anyway, more appealing destinations came through sailing in and out of a host of islands in the Caribbean; tramping through rain forests in Puerto Rico; many forays into various areas of Africa; getting into trouble in northern Thailand. This little episode ended in a stream of correspondence in verse, with Her Majesty's Custom Officers, Himself thinking it a great lark to include a mangy-looking mongoose in my carefully packed case. This did not stop our travels and soon we were gin-slinged in Singapore; avoiding spitting llamas in Machu Picchu. I was fascinated with a University-style lecture on its history by our personal guide whilst Himself was bored out of his skull with such academic attention he could have done well without – he preferred the spitting llamas. We've been agog in the Gaza Strip, listening to gun-fire from the Golan Heights en route to Bethlehem with a terrified Israeli Guide. Next day we were escorted into Israeli territory by an equally nervous Arab ex-military man – you would think they could have worked it out better, but for us it brought home the reality of their disparate lives. We travelled through Northern Ireland, too, during their troubles, went to Madagascar to see the lemurs. Bought a diamond ring in Turkey that cost more than the original build of the house that provided the funds for such wild extravagances. We've wandered through many islands in the Med; had a wee nosy into England; washed out in Wales; over-eaten in the United States; crossed Canada on the Blue Train and joined in the excitement of seeing the Aurora Borealis, although that was absolutely nothing on what we saw outside our own front door back in bonnie Scotland. We've experienced Zanzibar with all its intrigues; been fascinated by Myanmar though infuriated by the disregard to native fishermen as we sailed up the long approach of the Irrawaddy Delta to Rangoon, remembering my father had taken a ship in there during the second world war. We've been awe-struck in Egypt; seriously threatened in Casablanca and charmed in Mozambique by the friendliness of the police, after being warned of the dangers of this particular venture. There were other exotic destinations, yet my piece-de-resistance was surely our trip into the upper regions of the River Amazon. It was us two only with a crew of 18, a guide and the Captain of an old tub, built on the Clyde, some time in antiquity and showing serious signs of not being fit for purpose. We loved it, every nerve-wracking entertaining minute of it.

It took several crackling calls to convince him, yes, that is what I said! The Amazon! 'Russia,' he insisted. 'You said we were going to Russia.' Well, I *had* been looking into a trip to Russia that somehow turned into the Amazon. I had never been good at geography and a seriously researched plan to visit The Great Wall of China and a cruise on the Yangtze River saw us sailing round Mauritius and the Spice Islands.

Despite his initial shock at the prospect of rooting around the Amazon, this man who opted to leave control of our destinations to my vivid imagination, thought South America his favourite country. We had fantastic adventures on that trip, fighting not only the crew for the poor supply of food but a cantankerous parrot who would sneak very quietly up the leg of your chair whilst you were engrossed in ensuring you got a bite to eat, and snatch what was on your plate before taking off, squawking in delight. Pilfering food, being far from plentiful, earned him enemies among the crew who would serve bread with no butter, or butter with no bread, depending upon their own needs, which did come first. We, the valuable passengers, and the parrot, were well down the pecking order. But no matter how hungry, we never reverted to the parrot's sneaky tactics. For me, the favourite country had to be Africa, North, South and East, but not to date, the West.

Sometimes we took off on these long-haul journeys with just the mere two weeks leave Himself got off the rig, but he was always up for it. I would pack his bag as well as my own, meet him off the helicopter pad and head for some outward bound airport. Not a quiver of the anxiety that should have engulfed us, had we more sense. We had great faith in the vagaries of the weather as a mere delay of hours could have thrown our plans asunder. Him stuck on the rig for days and me pondering the wisdom of going off without him. Thank goodness it was a decision I never had to make. Never for a moment did we imagine the great British Travel Trade could have had one of its major tantrums and cocked up the whole caboodle like they do today!

Nor did we ever believe we might have caused concern, in particular to my mother, a born worrier, who came with Dad to look after the property, their young grandchild and whatever animals were about. On one occasion, with us en route home, my mother pacing the floor wondering at our lateness, eventually turned to a very young Neil, who was hanging over the back of the settee, waving his legs in the air. She wailed, 'What on earth can be keeping that ones?'

Showing not the slightest concern, he nonchalantly replied, without interrupting the rhythm of his wildly swinging legs, 'They're probably dead and buried by now!'

So we had no excuse for not knowing what was what in visitor expectations and how the rest of the world treated their tourists. We stayed at times in some of the top hotels before venturing forth into the unknown. Being a Gemini, I thrive on the chalk and cheese options in life, that being one of the main reasons I warmed to the variations of a seasonal job, one I was prepared to work – after an initial run-in of say, about five years of mucking about – every single day of the expanding season. Then have the winter off, so to speak. As off as I could make it before pre-bookings, marketing and a growing need for paperwork took over much of those precious months, along with the constant refurbishing required to keep up with my growing ambitions.

To this day, consternation is caused when I enthuse on the joys of January, which I love, it being the only time in the year I can truly snuggle down with a book in front of a blazing fire, draw the curtains at three o'clock in the afternoon and forget about the world.

Well, it used to be like that, before I acquired a boss.

3

As Green As I'm Cabbage Looking

'wow! that's pretty spectacular looking.' The building was massive, the dark background of the London streets of Whitehall emphasising its power. This was the Home Office in all its glory, lit up like a Christmas Tree. No one there of course. Just another instance of the government telling us all what to do to save energy, while they, being above their own edicts, are happily wasting more overnight fuel in heating and lighting empty offices than a whole community of homes could afford in an entire year.

Suddenly 'Go Green' became the main mantra in tourism. The devotees, zealous in their adoption of the green 'rather cross' code, hounding those of us with a modicum of scepticism and a fear that the cost of buying into the green scheme could be the death knell of a marketing budget. These were already staggering under the weight of all the components required to ensure our properties were legally blessed to showcase across the world. Some of the green supporters could be humourless in their demand that we all dip into our pockets and join up.

Before I was persuaded to don the colour, I sat beside a colleague with a similar view to my own, both of us keen to know the facts before doing something about it and listening intently to the earnest presentation before being overcome with mirth.

Probably the whole of the world knows by now that in 2005 the Scottish Tourism Board metamorphosed into VisitScotland, to the sound of much wailing and gnashing of teeth, both from the trade and the staff of the 14 autonomous Area Boards that covered Scotland under the auspices of the Scottish Tourist Board, who, according to some pretty vociferous members, had been doing a rotten job. That was until the government-driven threat of amalgamation into one single board called VisitScotland gave vent to an outcry over waving goodbye to our wonderful hard-working local area boards. And this to put up with a single entity that would never fill the sainted shoes of the previously much maligned Area Tourist Boards!

This transformation kept consultants in Jaguars for years, kept the anxious staff of the 14 boards (not to mention the one extra office over the border in London) on tenterhooks wondering what was to become of them. They were obliged to adhere to the governmental practice of enticing people into re-applying for their current jobs now to be gobbled up and spat out under new titles.

It turned the trade into serried ranks of those for change and those against. All riveting stuff involving much wavering of opinions, domination of opinions and, for the likes of me in my representative role, taking to the hills, that being the only place left to get away from opinions.

Some years down the line from that auspicious day when the government finally laid to rest its consultations, they did what they intended doing anyway and formed the mighty VisitScotland. The opinion this colleague and I sat listening to reduced us to smothering our giggles in an attempt to act our age, which was rather more than the delegate average, so we should have been setting a better example.

A 'green' man had been invited, indeed a top chap from the consultancy company working along with VisitScotland to deliver the knowledge on savings to be made, to the pocket and to the environment, by going green. He knew well in advance he would be speaking to some of Scotland's top bed and breakfast operators, a savvy audience and extremely smart in appearance – as is highly usual at tourism conferences. But by dint of the restrictions in bed capacity to no more than six guests to each establishment, it was impossible to achieve anything like the income he kept referring to in sums of six figures, allowing savings well beyond most of our annual turnovers, leave alone our profits.

Our man lacked conviction standing there spouting numbers relative to huge hotels, not small B&Bs, one side of his shirt tumbling over his trousers, the other tucked in, his entire appearance rather in need of a trim and brush up. His footwear had never come into contact with a lick of polish, nor his trousers with an iron. It was difficult not to be more amused than influenced.

The moment he finished, out of the audience flew a virago who wiped the floor with us. She was a zealous new convert, just receiving her Green Tourism Award and we felt suitably chastened for our adolescent behaviour. She was so steamed up she actually made a much better plea for the worthiness of joining the cause, so we did just that, in support of her spirited belief rather than the man paid to convince us!

Not long after that at another seminar which included the green issue, a friend sat with me and I whispered the story of the millions which gave us a less than attentive attitude as we listened to the green presentation. There was great emphasis put on the high emissions of CO_2 our industry ploughed into the atmosphere and how we must seriously consider mending our ways and stop encouraging those flights to our Highland Capital that had become the life-blood of the tourism spend in our sorely tried rural locations.

I had a sneaky feeling the presenter was less than impressed with my input during the question and answer session and at the end of our lecture, this little 'green' man bore down upon us and pointed one of his stern green fingers in my direction. 'See you two...' but I was ready this time and before he could say more, I countermanded his attack by pointing back a long white finger. 'It's not CU_2, its CO_2 that's the problem, and it's very worrying' I grabbed my friend and scarpered.

Anyone with sense, unless stupidly wasteful, can enter the scheme at Bronze Level, though it takes a bit more effort to reach Silver and Gold. However, many of the small B&Bs resent having to pay an annual subscription to continue doing what they always did, especially those with a seasonal income and small marketing budget.

At that time, the membership fee covered the 'green' man coming to see you, for hours, to bamboozle you with science. Some of it made sense, much of it was too much information, none of it was backed up in hard copy, which would have been very useful when you have a million other things to think about. Referring back, when necessary, would have been helpful had his verbal onslaught been confined to paper. You were then expected to spend more of your precious time keeping energy files and sorting out your past energy expenditure in pounds and units and whatever, keep ongoing records so you could prove year-on-year that you are saving the planet.

Your reward is a saving in costs if you put in lights so low your guests would need a guide dog to manoeuvre round their rooms. Or install those bright white flickering energy saving lights, adding dazzling new colours to the aura of colours so familiar to migraine sufferers, which sees them guzzling medication the pharmaceutical pundits put on the market by systematically destroying vast swathes of the environment in the need to research their products – or so the green lobby tells us. Or, if an hotelier with vast numbers off rooms, you can save a fortune by happily installing low levels of lighting forcing visitors to take paperwork into the loo to read in the brighter lights hopefully found there. Mark my word, one bright day a smart litigious American will sue the ass of us in recompense for all the bumps and scrapes adorning their precious body, once they get back to the USA and can actually see the damage in their bright shining artificially lit country. So, there are risks to going green.

One thing in my favour is our extensive use of fruit and household vegetables for the guests leaving a healthy compost heap bidding to turn my white fingers green. Added to which, masses of bottles and mounds of newspapers make an impressive contribution to the banks, giving the much-noticed impression I have little else to do with my life but drink wine and read papers.

And another interesting aspect, the Green Logo is supposed to give you the advantage of running a responsible establishment into which, if not our lackadaisical British tourist, then our conscientious Europeans will flock, lured by eco-friendly credentials, we are assured. On the other hand we have the Americans, some of whom can prove very awkward, giving us a hard time if they decide to keep away from us because they don't care about the environment and want only to stay in places where they can leave on the lights, fans, radios and televisions at all times. Where they can turn up the heating and open the windows, and complain we don't have air conditioning. Why? So they can leave that on too. So, there's good and bad in being green. For the time being I'm sticking at a sickly shade of yellow, until I know more!

It's all very well adhering to a strict green code, but what about the side effects of falling standards in facilities, in amenities and services to below an acceptable level? This had been voiced by many proprietors who find it difficult to increase prices to cover the more expensive local supply, especially when it comes to food. It takes a fair bit of water to make a place sparkle, to have pristine white sheets and towels, and to get a loo to flush away what not even the user wants to discover when innocently lifting a lid! The green desire to stick a brick in the cistern, to conserve water, is not a good idea unless you are the sole user of that particular loo. Or if the cistern has an extraordinary capacity that allows for the requisite amount of water to do the job properly and also accommodate the brick so loved of the green party in the early days of advice.

I, in my eager desire to do something green, stuck a brick into a large, old fashioned but very attractive, cistern. It lay there for years, saving the planet, until very recently, with new-found hours of idleness to hand, I decided to clean the cistern, inside as well as out! The kind of work an over-active brain finds for idle hands in the initial euphoria of having too much paperwork and too little physical work to do. I dropped the brick, cracked the cistern and failed to find a replica, it being a delicate shade of Arctic Blue long gone out of production! I had to have a cistern made, at considerable cost, not just money but time on the internet finding someone, anyone, who could help me out, and then had the total embarrassment of explaining to my insurers how I got into such a pickle. At least it gave them a laugh, which was not exactly the reaction from Himself when I tried to explain I was only following the green policy. Warning: don't put a brick in it to save the planet.

As for food, try following the carbon footprint of, for example a prawn; better travelled than myself in my hey-day. A trip out East just to be shelled, flown back home to our Scottish table to be eaten, then tell me how green that practice is. Yet that well travelled prawn will be cheaper to buy than the one fished out of the sea not a couple of miles from your fish monger! Ridiculous isn't it!

Sitting here as I write, the luxury of a laptop computer allowing me to enjoy a wonderful fire, bitter cold outside and cats inside, it's difficult to conjure the appropriate guilt I'm assured I should feel, for burning peat and logs on an open fire as the storm rages against window panes.

I appreciate I am in the company of several cats as I smile across at Skimbleshanks, black and white Smudge sitting on the arm of his chair smiling into his face with the same fervour she spits in the face of her daughter, Poodie-Pooh, hogging the mat in front of the fire. Meanwhile her brother Hobbit is convinced I enjoy the relentless kneed of his long, sharp, personal crampons. I almost howl with laughter when I hear yet another cat has entered the fray. Our own three miscreants now remonstrated with for venturing to join us by the fire when they should be in their beds in the kitchen, lectured the man I dubbed Skimbleshanks, the guardian cat of the railway train. To me, a very appropriate alias, considering his enthusiastic checking of my erratic working habits, far removed from his strict routine which never led to those panic-struck, heart-stopping moments when the possibility of a double booking met an unexpected visitor on the doorstep.

Now, listening to the evening news with Gordon Brown ramping up interest in green issues as he prepares to deliver to the nation his eleventh, and no doubt final, budget, green was very much on the agenda. It will be peppered with the word green, the bookies taking bets on exactly how many shades he mentions, but that is not what drew the laughter. It is the fact T S Eliot has a lot to answer for! Former Treasury mandarin Lord Turnbull, who worked with Gordon Brown for some years, has likened our man at No. 11 to Macavity, the hidden paw, the cat who is never there when the evidence of his crimes comes to light! An apt description!

Anyway, part of being green is being admirably knowledgeable on the wildlife in your area, a sentiment embraced by my enthusiasm for all things living. People too – not all of them – reluctantly conceding when cornered, that yes, animals by dint of necessity, do come first in a life or death honest-to-goodness answer to the tricky condemnation, 'You prefer animals to people, don't you?' This was flung at me in days gone by when my morning chores had, by necessity during lambing time, my unequivocal attention, regardless of family needs. My life was ruled by equine and ovine needs more urgent than any human requirements first thing of a morning! Guests or no guests, the animals came first.

The preparation and serving of all breakfasts had a priority structure that brooked no interference. First, food to the sheep, after the long arduous check involving all sorts of obstacles and hidey-holes to find the missing new mothers. This left me weak with exhaustion before I laid a hand to hauling the mountains of hard feed and hay to the long lines of wooden troughs which first had to be tipped over from their resting position keeping the inevitable rain out. During such exertions the sheep attacked from all directions flinging me to the ground so they could gobble up the spilled spoils and not have to wait politely in line as was expected of them.

The fact my guests did not quite behave in like manner at feeding times did not push them up the pecking order. I could spot a belligerent animal, usually too late, whereas people were much less predictable, the beatings emanating from my fellow men being of the verbal type, which somehow seems less forgivable than being pitched headfirst into a muddy pool then trampled upon with gusto. Sheep always managed to look indifferent to the chaos they painstakingly created when I eventually got to the feeding station, my innocent expectation of getting there and back in one piece totally annihilated. Being an optimist, I foolishly thought, today, they will behave. They never did, ever!

After feeding those woolly hooligans, it was on to my little hospital ward in the barn to visit and feed new mothers and ensure the cosseted lambs of yesterday have survived the night. After this the orphaned lambs had to be bottle fed, their eagerness making light of the chore, except for the sickly one that takes forever to persuade a trickle of milk down its reluctant throat while the rest of the sticky contents run up my reluctant arm. I worried about them, always. Time cracked on and the horses could be heard demanding to know why they are always relegated to last place. Their ability to neigh in unified defiance fit to waken all guests and neighbours alike, echoed out from their nearby stable. Impatient thuds could be heard as they take to emphasising their point with a hefty kick to the door. That meant Bronco, our escape artist, had managed once again to open his loose box and would be waiting to pounce on me from behind the stable door.

Then, back to the house, which often contained a house rabbit and the inevitable cats, at one time a dog, all queuing, all licking their lips in anticipation. Birds had to be fed, followed by any family or friends foolish enough to venture into the kitchen at that hour. They were usually the ones to suss out that animals came first as they slouched about looking grumpy whilst I happily tended my menagerie. Alas, as soon as it was time to feed the humans, I began to look grumpy as I dashed about preparing for the huge undertaking of guests' breakfasts, at one time ranging in number from 12 down to the six of recent years.

Me? Food is essential to my high metabolism, so I must have eaten, but never memorably so, when busy. When Himself was at home, and tended the larger animals according to our bargain hammered out in my *Heads on Pillows* days, my mornings were frittered away, having only the birds, the rabbit and the cats to tend before the precious guests. During lambing I often went out with him and, surprise, surprise, that flock of ill-bred vandals that gave me such a hard time, behaved like classy ladies of leisure. No attempts whatsoever were made to trip him up, throw their full weight against him from behind, or butt his bum when bending over, and you can't tip out a bag of feed without bending over. I've tried and it doesn't work. No, they kept all that fun and games for me because they knew I just love animals and would enter into the spirit of fun and games without the ability to get back at them. For them it was a case of, no dog, no stick, no sense! Himself always carried the crooked stick, and assured the flock I was his dog and my bite was every bit as good as my bark.

Now they are gone, the sheep, the horses, the rabbits, the dog; but expectations in breakfast menus and dining-room demands have grown to such proportions, it takes as long to feed six guests as it once did to attend that array of hungry mouths. Thankfully, despite the imperious behaviour of some guests, I'm no longer screamed at in high neighing tones to get on with it, nor do I get boxed onto all fours in a bid to get to the table in a hurry! Nevertheless, the animals seemed to find ways of involving the guests, with the blame placed at my door for all therianthropic behaviour, one thing being certain: there's a bit of the beast in all of us, and for sure, animals behave in ways we are apt to think the province of the human race.

Like the final day of the season last year. The Hobbit, our only boy cat ever, believes himself to be an essential component of entertaining the guests, despite my endeavours to ensure no cat goes into the lounge, guest bedrooms or the dining-room. He sussed out the fire doors long ago – all the cats do that – and nips through at the last second, whipping round the swiftly closing gap. On this particular day I met him in the hallway, heading for the dining-room.

'Take one more step in that direction, lad, and I'll bite your bum!' I warned.

'Oh,' came a voice from behind, a gentleman I assumed safe at the table. 'Is that my punishment for being late!'

Such repartee is part of the ambience of our home but many incidents involving animals very often left me with rather more egg on my face than on the plates I served!

4

Egg On My Face

DESPITE MY LOVE OF ANIMALS, and sincere attempts to be green, there were times when my wildlife knowledge fell way short of the mark. One afternoon, in our kitchen overlooking the braes where the big, fat, wild rabbits, spoiled by my protection from antagonists, enjoyed their main warren, we watched as a fox came down to the perimeter fence behind our house in pursuit of a juicy rabbit. Himself told me he had one day watched, mesmerised, as the very same fox crept almost up to our back green and as quiet as a mouse, snaffled a rabbit in the blink of an eye. The poor bunny didn't know what hit him. I remonstrated, on behalf of our latest house rabbit, Jettison. Those were her friends! I was firmly told to leave the wildlife to get on with what was natural to them and observe without interference.

Now I had the opportunity. This was as close as I ever saw Raynard on the land in daylight. The rabbit shot down a burrow. I cheered. The fox rampaged about for a bit then began, in the most aggressive manner, to dig at the burrow, hind quarters up in the air and front paws going like pistons.

It was a beautiful afternoon and the sun glinted off his russet rear, his fabulous brush bobbing up and down in his efforts to get at his prey. The grass on the braes, kept short by the nibbling of rabbits and cropping of horses and sheep, was sharp and green in contrast to his coat. The horses and sheep had moved pastures a good week before, so none disturbed the intensity of his ferocious attack on the burrow.

Despite the beauty of the hunter and his determination, I was rooting for the rabbit, but I think Himself hoped the fox would be the victor. Being married a long time now, we knew not to air our differences unless necessity demanded, so we watched, fascinated, in silence.

Raynard would dig a bit, stop, listen, then run a little to where another outlet must have been, ears intently forward giving his movements a fervour suited to a fox. Then back to the digging. He was convinced Peter Rabbit would pop out the other bolt hole, keeping more of an eye on it than the area of digging. He got more and more frustrated when this did not happen. Eventually, between bouts of digging and checking the bolt hole, he bit off chunks of turf in a towering rage, threw pieces all over the place, high into the air in his angst. Just when he moved to closely inspect the burrow's back door, Peter Rabbit shot out of the hole the fox had dug so wide. Up the hill raced Peter to the big warren, jet propelled, accompanied by my shouts of, 'Good on you, rabbit!'

I had kept silent long enough. Himself gave me a dignified dirty look.

This was one of my house-rabbit's pals, after all. The fox now had no chance, so deep was the main warren, and full of very large bold rabbits. I thought it quite hilarious; it certainly was not common to see a fox in the fields so close to the house.

A few days later, just after I had served breakfast to the guests and Himself was enjoying the comparative tranquillity of being back on his oil rig, there, on the top of the hillside, I saw Raynard. Gloriously red and so beautiful I just had to share the experience and ran through to the dining-room to announce his presence to a table of guests, now happily into their main course, all eight of them.

'Remember the fox I was telling you about? Well, he's back, lying on the top of the hill. I can't believe it. Usually they stay well away during daylight.'

The table rushed, en masse, through to the kitchen window to gaze at the fox, stretched out in the morning sun. His long brush could be clearly seen, though his head was not as visible as we would have liked, the land at the top of the brae being well covered by whin. They oohed and they aahed at this opportunity to see wildlife in the raw, not a thought to their rapidly cooling breakfast. After a few minutes of appreciative admiration, the fox made a leisurely stretch and languidly got to his feet. I gawked. Oh, no! It couldn't be. I spun towards the guests and enthused.

'Gosh! How wonderful is that, but your food will be getting cold,' I made lots of encouraging noises trying to shoo them back to the table, making sure I stood between them and the window. But no good.

'Oh, I think he's coming down the hill,' one woman excitedly whispered. 'I'll get the camera. I might get a shot of him.'

'No! Don't do that. The minute you open that door, he'll be off,' I assured as I anxiously herded them towards the dining room.

I prayed to myself that the great big fat orange pussy-cat from next door with the extraordinary bushy tail, would just clear off into the whins from which he had come. How could I make such a mistake! Glasses! Obviously the day was drawing near when I would have to address my creeping years!

The blessed creature must have heard me. It ever so quietly sidled into the abundance of undergrowth and the satisfied guests all trooped back to the table. But of course, by now, doubts cast aspersions at my failing eyesight. Did the guests genuinely appreciate this rural scene, or were they merely humouring me? Were they quietly shaking their heads? Probably more saw foxes in their urban gardens than I saw in my green wildness.

Did they recognise the red cat for what it was? I honestly do not know if they did, or did not, but such was my paranoia, I listened outside the dining room for whispers of, 'Don't tell the poor woman it's a cat. It will only upset her.' But if they did know, they hid it well and I am sure some of them at least would regale their next breakfast companions with their wildlife experience, whilst I have a sneaky feeling that others would relay the story of the silly B&B wifie who lived on the land and could not tell the difference between a marmalade moggy and a red fox!

On another occasion an otter strolled into view in the top patio, just sauntered out of the trees. Rarely did we see that elusive creature, so this indeed was one not to be missed. And it really was an otter! Not a dog, not a cat, but an otter, so close even I could not be wrong. I shot off for a witness.

No one in the lounge. Where was everyone when I needed them? Down through the fire doors to the sitting room. None there either so back into the bedroom corridor. 'There's an otter in the back garden,' I announced, ears pricked for a response.

That did it. A bedroom door flew open and I nabbed an innocent couple. In a flash we were back at the window with one poor soul, practically in his shirt tails, his wife tut tutting behind him. Of course, the otter was gone by the time we got there and none, not one single person would believe me, but it really was an otter, never seen before or since so close to home.

My latest faux pas I managed to keep to myself, it too bringing as much pleasure as the fox incident to those who believed. A few years ago we were wakened just the other side of midnight by screams.

I sat up in bed, eyes popping. 'Someone's being murdered.' Himself being deaf heeded me not. I listened, frozen and wide-eyed. The screams were awesome and fortunately not coming from the ground floor where all the guests slept. There actually had been a murder in a village not too far away, a male guest killing his female companion, so it happens, and they had stayed in a B&B, though the dastardly deed was carried out in woods nearby. There was plenty of speculation as to why but we never did know, the accuser taking his own life within his prison cell before the case came to court. The incident, despite its sensational grip on the neighbourhood, was soon forgotten.

Next night it was the same. Screech! Screech! filling the air during the early part of the night, and my gallant protector off back to his peaceful rig again! A fox, calling in the hills? I questioned the surrounding emptiness. Often I lay and listened to the alarming courting calls of amorous foxes as they strutted their stuff in the hills. But these new sounds did not quite have the eeriness conveyed by the fox.

Eventually we saw the elusive perpetrators. Owls! Large and

beautiful, they glided by the windows on occasions as they came and went from their habitat in the trees behind the house. They were a rare sight to us but Shane, out one day with his Dad, had the joy of seeing parent owls with their young. Their flight path took them past his house and they would stop and sit on the fences at times, resting between quartering the fields and soaring over the gulley that ran close to their home. We'd see them sometimes on a particular hill, flying close to the main road from the nearby town of Thurso to our village, as they circumnavigated their hunting grounds. Many of the guests had the pleasure of spotting them.

One tranquil light summer evening, as it can be in the northern hemisphere, about midnight, I determined to trace the screeching and see if I could spot where the owls were calling from. Exploring the direction of the sharp sounds I met a guest and explained my mission. She came with me and soon we were rewarded by the most graceful flying displays against the darkening sky as two owls flew in wheeling circles. Screeching calls were clearly heard, as if in response, coming from the trees.

'They must be out hunting and keeping in touch with their young,' I ventured, happy, despite the lateness of the hour, we had witnessed this rare display. We watched, fascinated, in the still of the night, hearing only the calls of the owls, before bidding each other good-night. Next morning my satisfied guest delighted her breakfast companions recalling the aerial display exhibition of the evening before.

That night several guests stayed up very late before the owls obliged once again. This time I watched with an intensity as, despite the very poor grey light that evening, there was something about the flight that differed from the gliding swoops I saw in daylight when the long-eared owls moved from their wooded cover out into the open.

My guests were enthralled as the same two birds of the previous evening, one smaller than the other, swooped and swirled giving out weird screeching calls. I peered intently. Oh, no! Not again. Sighing heavily as shadows gathered, I watched the birds become much more owlish in their appearance but I hung my head in shame, vowing never again to entice guests into thinking they saw what they did not see. For now I knew who exactly our sky divers were and if I got caught out on this one, I really would never live it down.

Years before, a young boy and his family stayed with us every year, their passion for fishing bringing them back with catches they gutted round the back of the house where we had a convenient water tap. This attracted a young seagull we never particularly noticed until after Lee grew up and found other interests, the gull continuing to visit us every April, hanging about until disappearing around August. She demanded food, and Connie, having a greater passion for animals than even I had, fed her kippers and herring and all sorts of goodies. Eventually Kee-Har, called after Peter Adam's gull in Watership Down, demanded her rights by parading on our window sill and bashing the window if we tried to persuade her this was behaviour beyond the pale and would not be tolerated. We had yet to learn who was boss when it came to seagull determination.

Our Kee-Har was a female herring gull, unlike Peter Adam's male black-back, his much smaller and neater with a wide and interesting vocabulary accentuated by a strong patois of Continental origins. Ours was definitely a Scottish no-nonsense herring gull and raised her voice to remonstrate whenever necessary, Gallic charm being the last thing on her mind, though I suspect a smattering of Gaelic swear words. She grew huge on her diet of fish from the table as well as directly from the sea, always gleaming white and quite beautiful. The guests were fascinated when catching glimpses as she spread her massive wings on the sill, or stood there demanding attention whilst covering my clean window panes with a beak-wielded gunk that defied removal. She had little or no fear of us and kept all other gulls at bay, even the much smaller and decidedly better mannered bird we believed was her mate as we saw them billing and cooing on a neighbour's chimney. The Sheiling was her domain and woe betide any other gull who showed interest.

One of our kittens, Poodie-Pooh, a bold little madam, once grabbed Kee-Har by the leg and was hoisted into the air while I frantically shouted to Poodie to let go. She did, eventually, earning a solid thump after an alarming drop from her involuntary flying lesson.

Now I was mortified, convinced the aerobatics were performed by Kee-Har and her boyfriend. It was difficult to tell for sure because we also had a pair of curlews nesting on the bog land that formed part of our apportionment. No way could you see in this half light against the darkening sky if the birds were white or the light buff colour of the owls and the curlews. Did seagulls display and give unusual calls at midnight? Eventually everyone wandered back to the house, pleased with their night's entertainment. Would they have stayed up to see a couple of seagulls fool around? I don't think so.

At least it was not they who suffered further wildlife extravaganzas at the hands of Shane when shadowing me early one summer morning as I prepared breakfast for a table of six.

The tale of the mouse actually began the day before, at a seminar on taxation. By then I was involved in many aspects of developing 'the tourism product' in areas across Scotland and was keen small B&BS would have every opportunity to find out just how the taxman went about his business. More and more bed and breakfast operators were being, what many saw as, victimised into expensive and demoralising investigations into their earnings. Those who got the dreaded brown envelope of intent were the very people who were actually declaring their income. It was galling for them to receive this when well they knew of many others who neither declared income nor joined any tourism organisation. They were virtually getting their business on the backs of those who were being investigated and in all probability, put a high percentage of their income into marketing the area to bring visitors to doors. Visitors that often ended up in the beds of others when there were too many heads for the pillows offered through expensive websites, brochures and other forms of advertising.

It was, after all, they who were investing a portion of their earnings marketing with the Tourist Boards, the AA, or whoever, paying for advertising that enabled these agencies to raise the profile at home and abroad putting small areas on the map. Nothing really could be done about non-joining establishments picking up the business because they were in a more lucrative position despite others paying to show to the world that these more isolated areas existed. This enabled a neighbour to cock a snoop, declaring they didn't need the tourist boards and all that entailed, in reality meaning, why pay when I can get it for nothing! But someone had to pay to bring the visitors to the area in the days before individual websites could be credited with doing their bit.

That was bad enough for the conscientious member, but the members also made themselves sitting ducks into the bargain. It was easy for Her Majesty's Revenue & Customs officers, when pushed for something to read in a tea break, to pick up the mainline tourism brochure and say, 'Hey, do you think Mrs So-and-so in Nowheres-ville is declaring her B&B? She's bound to be earning a bob or two. Let's check her out. Months of easy work here, pal. She'll no attack us with distinguished council or silver-tongued lawyers, distressing our days, will she?'

Ah, but Mrs So-and-so from Nowheresville has an accountant and believes herself to be beyond reproach. Meeting the notification of investigation with reasonable confidence is no measure of the pain awaiting her during something like nine months to a year later. If Mrs So-and-so still manages to hold on to her sanity, she's of a different frame of mind completely, after every little penny that wormed its way through her accounting system is scrutinised. Then she must account for the pennies the taxman believes *must* have entered into her life, but not her books! Passports, bankbooks, cheque books, as well as every conceivable receipt for every penny ever spent must be found or answered for. It is a chastening and totally demoralising experience as any will testify, all of whom thought they were running an honest and up-front business. One friend received her brown envelope on Christmas Eve intimating the intention to investigate her accounts. At least HMRC did not have the audacity to add Merry Christmas!

Yet, at the end of a very long and arduous time, most are told they do not owe a penny to their country, and some actually get a rebate! Of too little significance to make up for the hassle involved, to be sure, and in reality more annoying than if the taxman were owed something.

So, our friend from the tax office, and he was indeed friendly, had us hanging on his every word during his presentation. The following extraction, from the monthly tourism column I write for the *Northern Times* gives a more accurate account of our day than I can now remember, and no, I'm not off on a tangent; it does tie up with mice:

A Taxing Situation

In this country, you are innocent until proven guilty, except, it appears, when your guilt is of a fiscal nature. At a recent seminar, a tax advisor smugly announced, 'As far as the Inland Revenue is concerned, you are guilty until you prove yourself innocent!' Nero at least had the excuse of madness when he decreed that the guilt of the Christians could be presumed!

'But surely you must bring suspicion upon yourself first,' we chorused. Apparently not. Suspicious returns will certainly set the taxman at your heels, but our friendly tax advisor has another ploy up his sleeve to snare the unsuspecting. He picks your name out of a hat, or ways to that effect, and assuredly, it is as random as that, to fall foul of a tax investigation.

'That means you investigate only those who put in returns, and are totally up-front,' we howl in derision, the full implication of being honest dawning upon us. 'What about the people who never declare an income? They stick out signs and never pay a penny towards attracting visitors to the area. You surely can't mean you only investigate people who declare their income?' We were aghast at having this confirmed, and flabbergasted at what followed. 'We don't have the time or the resources to chase after these people, in fact, we rely upon you to report such instances to us.' In effect, an excellent charter for encouraging tax evasion. Or does he know, the same as you and I, that the profit from letting a couple of rooms for the short height of the season would fall far beneath a taxable level of income, unless, of course, another job is being held down too, as it often is.

Whatever way you look at it, it does seem very unfair that you can keep correct records and give correct returns, yet be subjected to months of misery while the taxman uses his mighty resources to try and nail you, and if failing to get his pound sterling, then he certainly gets his pound of the stuffing that's been knocked out of you while you jump through his hoops. It's no skin off his nose that you must still give hospitality with a happy, cheery grin on your face every morning, while you ponder the next set of queries he has in store for you. Just be thankful he is merely after your money and not, like Claudius Ceasar Nero, ready to feed you to the lions, even though you may well feel you've been dragged into the lion's den.

Many of these random investigations come to a conclusion that no fraud has occurred, and some even find in favour of the accommodation provider who has the satisfaction of a small cheque in the post. But it seldom covers the amount you may have to pay your accountant to service this investigation. That is why a number of proprietors have taken out membership of The Federation of Small Businesses, who will act upon their behalf, should their name pop out of the hat. This is at no further cost than membership fees, and there are, of course, other benefits to derive from joining the FSB. So beware, the taxman cometh, but the problem is, he cometh quicker for some than for others, and for the really guilty, he seldom comes at all.

A couple of days later, a letter arrived from an accountant assuring me he was a keen reader of my column but I must not encourage my colleagues to rely upon going it alone or using only the services of the Federation of Small Businesses if caught in a tax investigation. In fairness to his beliefs, next month I wrote the following into which I was able to tell the tale of the mouse which occurred the morning after the first seminar:

More Taxing Demands

It was heartening to get feed-back from an accredited accountant, reiterating information given in last month's column on Inland Revenue investigations. However, concern was expressed that it may not be in a person's best interest to use the insurance cover provided by the Federation of Small Businesses (FSB) to handle a tax investigation in order to save fees incurred by an accountant.

This accountant believes a person would be better served by using their own accountant who knows their business personally. Emphasis is placed on the fact an FSB representative, who in all probability will be a stranger to the business, may conclude the investigation without meeting either the client or the Inspector of Taxes. He considers it prudent for the client to meet the investigating inspector at the earliest possible opportunity, a meeting which could prove vital to the final outcome. All very convoluted and taxing in itself to even think about. Being totally aware and using one's own discretion as to which is the best option makes sense, but for the many micro-businesses that do not employ an accountant, the Federation can be of invaluable help.

In a lighter vein, the following is further information given at the same tax seminar – food for thought!

This particular quirk of the taxman met with considerable indignation. He believes Bed & Breakfast operators have all the time in the world and encourages them to do a double shopping each time they meander to the supermarket. Why? It would be much easier for him to calculate his due if operators were to shop separately: one lot of food for the families, another for the guests. B&B people have loads of space too, he thinks, insisting upon separate store cupboards, with all the time in the mornings to cook separate meals for family and guests.

If you don't adopt his methods, then don't use his idiosyncrasies to dodge cooking a tasty morsel for a member of the family or you may end up like me, with more egg on your face than on the plate. This actually happened.

Cooking breakfasts for guests, small grandchild interrupts, 'Can I have a sausage?'

'No! The Taxman wouldn't like it,' he is told, thoughts of the previous day's talk on taxation uppermost in mind.

'Are they all for the Taxman?' the child asks.

More like for the bin if the taxman had his way, and everyone wants fish the following day, fresh local ingredients like these sausages should be chucked out – to keep the accounts as correct as intimated in his talk on how accuracy could be accounted.

'Can The Hobbit have one then,' the child persisted.

'No! The Hobbit is on the books as a Mouser, and his food must be kept separate – in a separate cupboard!' Sarcasm was taking over from contempt at such ridiculous fiscal expectations.

'Does he have to keep all his mice for the Taxman?' asked the child, eyes wide with wonder.

'What a good idea,' says I, losing patience. 'Now go out and play.'

Twenty minutes later, said child bursts into the dining room where I am removing plates in a quiet dignified manner, my guests that morning being of the loftier type. Brandishing aloft a decapitated mouse, gently swinging from its firmly held tail, Shane howls, 'Gwanny', as all eyes follow the swaying rodent. 'The Hobbit was eating the Taxman's mouse!'

Try explaining that one to the gagging guests.

In searching out these extracts, I found another reason to recall with a smile a short anecdote taken from an incident with guests. The phone rang and the caller identified herself as the couple we were expecting. 'We are at Eezo and we do not know how to find you.' The voice had a strong foreign accent, so I asked, 'Thurso? You are at Thurso?'

'No, we are at Eezo, the town of Eezo. There is a church spire I can see. We are at the outskirts, at a garage.

'Are you sure it isn't Thurso? It sounds like Thurso?' I insisted, ready to give directions.

'No!' she was adamant. 'I see the sign and it says E-s-s-o!' she declared triumphantly, spelling it out. It took some time to persuade her this was not the sign to a town but the large forecourt Esso sign as you entered the town of Thurso!

And now, here I am staring my last season in the face, 40 years in the making, packed with such incidents and so much information to impart to those who care. Himself is now champing at the bit to get our next house off the drawing board and onto the ground, to be built in the area where the rabbit dodged the fox, with views even better than here, if that is at all possible. Yet, it was he who wanted to continue doing bed and breakfast for longer, not to pull the plug entirely at the end of this season.

But you cannot really do that, linger on, playing at it. You have to know so long in advance that you'll not be buying marketing opportunities for the following year, that you will not require the services of the advisors who now take the place of the inspectors of old. How much of it shall I miss?

Certainly not the inspectors of old, *that* I can say with alacrity.

5

An Inspector Calls

THE IDEA WAS, you were not to know, prior to the big surprise in the morning, that such a person was in the area leave alone spending the night under your roof while you innocently go about the business of your trade, totally ignorant of the fact you are being spied upon.

As if!

In the mornings, the docile go along with the charade in droves, if not quite feigning delight then managing pleasant surprise, hearing the credentials of the strange guest, lurking about like a lingering party-goer after everyone else has gone home. Obviously waiting for other guests to depart the premises so he, or she, can pounce.

This of course was a dead give-away, should any doubts linger. Most guests who are still on the premises by 11.00am buzz about between lounge, bedroom, car, dining room, garden, whatever, but the inspectors incarcerated themselves in their rooms with the odd sneak out to see if the coast is clear. That cautious furtive look round the door always gave the game away. Otherwise we may have thought the guest back in bed of a morning, garnering a black mark. They could stay in bed at home. Why waste money staying in bed instead of getting out into the beckoning countryside, and more to the point, why upset the paid help's apple-cart when he could have their linen in the washing machine! My help would say it was more to the point he wasn't paid, but that did not stop the tendency towards getting upset when a guest returned to bed for the best part of the morning, crawling out bleary-eyed about noon, if you were lucky. Their other half would always be marching about like a time bomb ready to explode, waiting for their spouse to appear so they could make the best of their holiday. I had nothing but sympathy for both of them, knowing the vagaries of being in a relationship with someone from the opposite end of the planet in likes and dislikes.

It is when seeing the head poke round the doorway doing its stealthy check we anxiously enquire, 'Are you all right? Is there anything I can get you?' Prudent indifference to this unusual behaviour was one of the many requisites of fulfilling your end of the bargain when the inspector called. Naturally, the inspector did not collude in this little pantomime that had no effect upon the standard of services given anyway, this all-important gauging of standards of service and facilities being the reason for the visit.

If the easy-going went along with it, assuming shocked surprise, the belligerent met the triumphant presentation of the identity card with, 'I knew who you were anyway!' which was suicidal if the inspector took umbrage. Invariably the inspector would sweetly reply, 'Oh, if only you had said so, we could have cleared the air last night. That would have been much the better thing to do,' the sweetness of the smile assuring you're off on the wrong foot.

There were those who took advantage of the bush telegraph and went to great lengths the day before the overnight visit, racing about transporting plants from one premises to the next. Goodies appear in bedrooms never seen for the rest of the year, and comfort in public areas never known on other nights, with staff, to their great amusement, put on high alert best behaviour.

Even those of us who gave the best at all times had to affect surprise at the proudly flourished business card, after the bill was paid and you were feigning your cheery goodbye. Thereafter followed two hours of your undivided attention to him, or her, as the case may be. Though in the beginning, for me, it was always a she, and many years into such appearances before I could say I got one I could honestly say

I felt was a genuinely nice person. That was just not the way they came across in the very early years, when doing their job. However, I have no doubt their job had as much to do with my opinion as their personality, or lack of it, but I emphasise, that was in the raw beginnings of 'an inspector calls'.

Today is quite a different kettle of fish, although some insist it certainly is not! They who complain about the inspector's – or as we now say, the advisor's – visit, have no idea how the visit has evolved from the bad old days. For years now our advisors have been pussy-cats, in comparison that is, although the pussy-cats get a much better response to their well-thought suggestions and helpful hints than in the beginning. Certainly the faults did not all lie with the inspectors, not in my case anyway. It was a long and arduous learning curve for us all.

Most hotels, though very few B&Bs, were in membership with the Automobile Association, so the majority of visits to B&Bs were from the Scottish Tourism Board and of course, it was a new game to them too. It must have been the training, or possibly lack of it, that programmed these people to come into your home behaving in an arrogant and high handed manner. I suppose it was in order to cope with what was an extremely difficult job – there is no doubt about the difficulty, and there was no doubt about the arrogance of some inspectors. To point a home owner in the right direction required tact and good guidance, rather than veiled threats of 'you're out on your ear if you don't see it all my way'. Mind you, threats could come from other people, some pretty stroppy Tourism Information officers, which is unheard of today. I know because I was the recipient of such ire, though never told by an inspector to reconsider my attitude!

What had I done? I told a visitor, who had been sent to spy on me, to quiz me about staying at a place nearby, 'Sorry, I wouldn't put a dog there!' or so I was accused of and yes, I had said words to that effect. The visitor had a dog, a nice Collie dog, not that the dog was implicit in the ruse. Dogs, especially Collie dogs, have a much fairer attitude to life. I told you it was all about attitude and this amusing little ruse came from the attitude of mean-spirited proprietors, and was not the only time such weird behaviour occurred in the hope of catching out a so-called competitor.

I would have been a complete idiot to fall for such a practice, this particular play-act was much easier to see through than next time it happened, years later and with unbelievable effort, all to no avail. Twitchy proprietors indulging in such shenanigans were the owners of a poor product and if they spent as much time caring for their guests as they did trying to destroy the opposition, they too would fill their beds!

At that time I was delighted to take dogs, before the cat who replaced Felix put a stop to such heathen practices, but the place this woman was asking if I would recommend most decidedly did not take dogs, which I pointed out. I was full up, but if she was prepared to leave her dog in the car, then give it a go. I thought her persistent questioning was because of my heinous suggestion to consider leaving the dog in the car, that idea being anathema to dog lovers, who in years to come would give me a right dressing down for such a cruel suggestion. She headed off with her tail-wagging dog and before I knew it I was reported to a friend of that proprietor who was a TIC officer. I got a solid telling off, more for thinking it hilariously funny than the easily explained dog business. Humour was not always the best medicine when it came to avoiding the attacks of the few. In my case there were only two places that would sooner indulge in upping the anti than get along with the many others who worked together. I tried, boy I tried, to include all before telling myself to accept defeat. I'm kind of thick when it comes to accepting that some attitudes are deliberately derived through the inability of the person to share, and sharing became an essential part of changing competitors into colleagues and retaining friends when you happened to be doing much better than them.

For those of us who loved to work together, there were many ways of being alerted to the impending visit from the inspector if you did not hear serious suspicions on the grapevine.

The phone would ring and an anxious voice gasp, 'Have you an I. N. Hindsight booked for tomorrow night?' Quick glance at the register affirmed this. 'Oh, god. I knew it! He's from the tourist board. He just booked in here and, of course, with me being used to taking singles, I never twigged, but the minute I set eyes on him, I just knew!'

'Do you think they have a certain look, or can you smell their air of victory as they size you up?' I asked seeing if I could get her to laugh, but she was too far gone in anxiety to be humoured.

'You know fine. The clothes. The briefcase. The wee overnight bag. The eyes everywhere. Twitching to rub a finger over the furniture. Who else is like them! I wouldn't be surprised if that fellow has a white glove in his briefcase, to check the surfaces! Not a smile on his face. He doesn't like it here, never seen a sight of him all night which is so annoying, everyone else was in the lounge having a lovely time. Does he know that? No. Stuck in the bedroom as usual. I wish they wouldn't do that.' And that was her before the inspection.

Being caught off guard, in the morning, could give rise to chaos in the hectic time-table of clearing breakfast, stripping rooms, getting on with the mounds of washing, sorting out guest lounge and dining room, preparing dinner for new arrivals and every other time-consuming chore that had to be accomplished if you did not employ staff. Not to mention any intended shopping, getting in the precious fresh local food they banged on about so much. What if you had an appointment with your accountant, bank manager, even the dreaded tax inspector? All would have to be abandoned if there were no staff to take over. And of course, not employing staff, meant there was none other than yourself to blame when a piece of fluff was found, or worse, a hair! Aaaaaaahhhrrrr!

A neighbour who ran a large establishment as clean as the proverbial sixpence told me she got severely rebuked when the inspector found a hair in a drawer, advising her to have a word with her housekeeper. She had no hesitation in answering that had it been her housekeeper who had cleaned the rooms that day, there would have been no hair, but she had done that room herself! Had an inspector wanted to, they could reach up high and find dust in the cleanest of establishments, or search every drawer until they found what they were looking for. One look at bathroom porcelain, especially a shower, soon tells you just how clean the place is. Indeed, you know shortly after entering the premises and it is not the first time the tourist board lost a member because of the constant seeking for dust instead of taking heed of general good cleanliness, good food, ambience, a happy welcoming manner and provision of what makes a great night's stay in a bed and breakfast.

Which reminds me. Escorting my inspector to a bedroom in those first years, she instantly removed the heavy made-to-measure cover and with a flourish, demolished the made-up bed until she reached the bare mattress. This could have been accomplished in a room vacated by guests with bed already in a state of chaos, but no. The attack was made on a made-up room.

She then peered closely at the quilted structure of the mattress and began to scrape with her nail at the small indented buttons securing the material. I wondered afterwards if a good strong thumb-nail was a requisite of the job.

I peered as intently as her wondering what we were looking for until I just had to say, 'Okay, I give up. What is it we're looking for?' Of course, I should have maintained the well-known silence so much better to adopt on these rounds, rather than gabble through nerves, as had happened during my first visits. I thought I was learning the ropes but this was quite new to me. Linen inspected yes, and comfort of beds, yes, but this?

She moved to another cushioned depression. 'We do have to check how often you vacuum your mattress,' she impatiently informed me whilst coming up with the tiniest bit of fluff. 'There,' she triumphed, vindicating her bizarre behaviour in a room with impeccable bed linen and top of the range bed, obviously aspiring to the greatest of comfort and cleanliness.

'Oh dear me,' I commiserated, 'that is disgraceful. I wonder how I missed that.' I put as sorrowful a look on my face as my horse Bronco contrived when he deliberately stood on my toes to enliven particularly boring sessions of grooming.

But the sarcasm was lost on her, not having near as good a sense of humour as that horse in his hey-day. In fact, inspectors were bereft of humour in those days, indeed, only few of the many I have had enter my portals, showed what we would call a cracking sense of humour and again, I blame the job. One was a lovely person in every respect and from meeting her, an inspector would be the last job you would place her in, with her sparkling eyes in a particularly pretty face. She has now retired from a top position as an advisor with VisitScotland, and is running an excellent B&B herself in the Central Belt, that richly rewarded area of Scotland you have to work with if you want to have any real impact on what goes on in tourism. She is one of the nicest people you could come across and how she landed in such a job I will never know! Even more puzzling, she loved it!

The other was a gentleman, as close to the top of the tree as you can get in the inspection game, also just retired from VisitScotland and greatly missed by all. He too had charisma and that way of helping people achieve what they hoped would be theirs in the rankings that mattered so much when money was spent on advertising. I'm sure a rating was never given by either unless it was deserved, but they had that elusive correct attitude that served both their clients and the Tourist Board well.

Many of the problems that did arise stemmed from the inspectors not appreciating that the trade was as much their client as the visitor. It was in their client's best interest to ensure that all was well for the visitor. But, for the system to work, the visitor had to know the value of the higher ratings and it was up to VisitScotland, as the Tourism Board became, to get that rating known across the world. This, of course, made it all the more imperative that the trade acquire the higher ratings, provided their establishments lived up to it, which was all well and good. Competitiveness to ensure you had marketable facilities living up to visitor expectations was admirable. Being hell bent on getting the highest possible rating so you could swank to colleagues was not – and an awful lot of it went on!

My lady of the scraping nail had a long way to go before she could ever reach a light bit of banter, never mind risking humour on the job. However, it was not she who took exception to the way my drapes hung one morning.

I think this early day inspector thought she was being helpful as she had admired the material and the quality as well she might, all such drapery was made to measure by MacKenzies and any who dealt with them knew what that cost! But because such quality lasts and when chosen well seldom went out of fashion, in the long run it probably saved money. As with the Axminsters and Wiltons we put down in the public areas, the initial outlay being well worth the sacrifice of many a holiday.

As ever, I knew who my austere guest was and was glad she had not entombed herself in the bedroom, but came out into the lounge for a bit of a chat. I was a wee bit taken aback at her rather scruffy appearance, a none too pristine blouse and a grey-black, loosely gathered skirt with crumpled cream cardigan. At night, before dinner was even prepared, it was vital for me to don the smartest of apparel or I would not have felt comfortable – probably because my working clothes were well rubbed at the knees and my guests all made a point of returning early for dinner, so they could spruce up. She, however, did not see the need.

In the morning, on confirming her credentials, we did the rounds and when we came to her room I was chastised that though I had sufficient coat hangers, not one had the requisite slots with which she could hang up her skirt! She was right, the point being well made, but the said skirt was well crushed before she ever set off for her room. When she later climbed upon a dining-room chair to show me exactly how the swaging should hang on the curtains, her black skirt was covered in the white hairs of her canine companion, making her appearance all the more remarkable, this inspector who had no hesitation in having opinions contrary to her looks.

Himself was kept well out of the way of any inspector, usually on the oil rig and therefore seldom heard the stories doing their rounds. Little if anything of any problems I had in those early days reached his ears, in the belief what he didn't know wouldn't hurt, isolated as he was and unable to do anything but worry, should I convey my angst in a tantrum over the phone. However, in a spell on-shore, he took belligerent exception to being helpful in the run up to the inevitable annual inspection, which this time had been made by appointment, as were all visits not requiring an overnight stay.

Our exterior paint-work was then a rusty shade of red. I would much have preferred forest green and got in the paint, noticing that the drop-down steel garage door was more than a little worse for wear. The garden and exterior came under the inspector's remit, which had been pointed out to me the year before, but a whole year had passed in which to prove my good intention of repainting the garage door.

Himself had every intention of doing the job as he's an exceptionally tidy man and governed by high standards, until I foolishly told him the inspector's criticisms! Time was something he never had much of, with croft work building up in his many absences from home, but maintenance was vital and every other job was carried out the minute necessity arose. His kitchen garden was immaculate, no vegetable daring to step out of line, whilst my cottage-style flower garden was a bit of a riot, not so much of colour as of random planning with the odd weed to cheer things up.

Time was found for all else under his jurisdiction, but sadly, not the garage door. No way! He didn't have to face the inspector. I did, and got more and more anxious as the day drew near and Himself became highly defensive of his garage door.

Worse still, he was at home on the day of the visit and I primed myself for a drop in marks, so in order to maintain the overall high mark already gained, I made darned sure everything else was fit for a king, never mind an inspector.

The inspector came and he went, and never a mention of garage door. Himself did as he always did: kept well out of the way. Inspectors may be even more scary than guests!

On seeing what was actually my first male inspector off the premises, there was Himself, garage door hoisted up, car in garage with bonnet up, placed with engine area well and truly under the door as if gaining light from the bright sunshine. Who but a moron would ask him to move the disabled vehicle so he could bring down the door for inspection! My wily husband took his nose out of the engine, not a place his nose was usually to be found, wiped his hands, and was charm itself to the inspector.

My heart leapt though, as my inspector glanced up at the overhead door. 'I noticed on your score sheet you were due maintenance. Did you paint the garage door?' he said to Himself while I kept remarkably quiet.

'Oh, yes,' my husband agreed, smiling broadly. 'A very necessary job.' I couldn't believe my ears.

Later, I pounced. 'How could you tell a lie like that!'

Indignant, he gave me one of his looks. 'I'm not in the habit of telling lies. That man said, did you paint the garage door. Well I did, not that long after I built the garage! And it will get another coat of paint when I say so, not when he says so!'

Having made his point, very soon after, we had a lovely dark green garage door to compliment other areas of dark green paintwork about the premises.

His next brief encounter with the tourist board came when he was officially part of the team that delivered the goods and he felt it his bounden duty to accompany me on that never to be forgotten tour of the house. I still catch my breath in relief that blows were not exchanged that memorable day.

He, akin to our guests, believed we had everything necessary in perfect working order, that any good establishment should have, and much more to boot, but our crowning glory was always the hospitality and abundance of locally sourced quality food with lots of home baking to welcome people upon arrival. Neither he nor the guests understood that inspectors felt they were not doing their duty properly if they could not come up with some form of open debate as to the workings of the facilities. Although to be honest, I have not had such for years and to be more than honest, there were times that such criticism was well merited and taken the right way, helpful to progress. But you had to have a frame of mind that accepted this. You had to have the right attitude. I had. Himself had not.

Having felt the tensions build during the long visit, I said a grateful goodbye and leaned against the door. 'What on earth was wrong with you?' I demanded. 'There were times I thought you were going to explode!'

He no longer fumed quietly. 'Another minute and I would have floored that man.' That man happened to be from the AA not the Scottish Tourist Board and in my entire career the AA came across as being much easier to please. But Himself never had the pleasure of accompanying an inspector round his home before, and it showed!

'Oh, that would have been fun. One way to put this place on the market. I'll say one thing. You'd have had lots of plaudits from some in the sector, no doubt. But you would also have had a term behind bars to cool your heels!'

'Who the hell did he think he was, scrutinising perfectly clean beds, sniffing into that and peering into this. Peering up fans and down loos!'

'He was doing his job! And what's more, he was a nice man and I liked him!'

'I could tell you liked him, otherwise you'd have left-hooked him!' I'd never left-hooked anyone in my life, if I was going to start, now seemed like a good time, but I was far too exhausted and weak at the knees with relief that the visit was over and the inspector had escaped intact.

After that I kept my quiet man well away from inspectors, but, surprise, surprise, he took to his Skimbleshanks role with a new vengeance after picking up a trick or two from the inspector. Vacuuming overhead fans; running fingers over the tops of doors; remonstrating with me the moment he spotted a cobweb; demanding, was this done, was that done, because you never knew the minute you could have an inspector staying, became his habit, never mind what the guests expected.

'An advisor,' I would remind him. 'That's what they are now. And what you are now is a pain! I've done this job all these years and take it as normal when inspectors call; if not you just wind yourself up no end. What's good for my guests is good enough for any advisor, and for you too, so stop trying to complicate matters!'

'It's a good job they're in it. I can see it takes more than me and Shane to keep you on your toes!'

And he was right. It has to be said that without the guidance of good inspectors keeping us on our toes, I do not believe standards would have been driven up to meet the needs of today's discerning visitor in many places including my own, no doubt. Many decry VisitScotland, saying they do not need them. Actually, it's the visitor to this country who really needs them, and they serve that visitor well.

In those early days, the market was mainly domestic, coming from various areas of Britain, travelling in larger groups, particularly families. You could almost take for granted you would be turning away dozens of people in a night, pre-bookings being something I knew nothing of for many years after that 1968 start. Stories of sleeping in cars, specially opened public halls, and guests wanting to sleep in lounges, circulated all too frequently. You filled your rooms from this steady stream and if your visitors liked it, with no pre-bookings to hinder, they stayed on for days on end. Depending upon your outlook, such abundance was very often not an incentive to driving up standards. Those who preferred to pocket the money and get off with ploughing as little back into the so-called business were on a roll. They were literally laughing all the way to the stock-pile under the mattress, that comfortable lump all B&B operators were suspected of sleeping on.

The rest of us, who wanted to give the very best, not just to enable higher tariffs, but for pure job satisfaction, had a struggle to make ends meet. Prices charged and generosity given made it difficult to earn a genuine living in the B&B sector, unless you had a serious number of rooms on offer. Most people did not, especially in the rural areas.

It was to that purpose the Local Enterprise Companies came into the tourism sector with their remit of encouraging product development, and in their early days, to be part of the marketing of the economically sound businesses the area needed. If the tourist board got a fair amount of stick from its members, that is nothing to what the enterprise companies came in for when they too were seen not to come up to expectations. They were accused of nailing their money to the office floor in the face of many appeals to support schemes that could well have flourished, or just as easily floundered. Decisions were as difficult to make as people were to please. Rumour and innuendo gave some innocent personnel columns of bad press, and unscrupulous applicants the greatest opportunity to come into enterprise supported areas and have some pretty hare-brained schemes funded. It was fortunate that some staff were able to spot the winners, who made inward investment beneficial to our areas.

This was a good time to be driving forward anything to do with the tourism industry. A steady stream of visitors could be relied upon and the opportunity to meet with like-minded people helped put excitement into the product as you got together, courtesy of the enterprise companies and the tourist boards, exchanging ideas and supporting those around you, trying to make sure everyone delivered a good product in homes, restaurants, hotels, farms and shops, with the growing recognition that tourism is everyone's business.

6

The Camels Are Coming
O-ho O-ho

HAD THE INCESSANT DEMAND of the telephone come a mere few seconds later, I would have allowed the new-fangled answerphone to pick up the call. Had I done that, I would not have been viewed with doubting scepticism by my prospective guest as she backed out the door whilst a subtle battle was enacted by her travelling companion to persuade her to stay so they could see this camel for themselves. After all, such opportunities on the north coast of Scotland did not often come their way.

The crackling line, courtesy of our much-in-need-of-upgrading local exchange, did not surprise, nor did the sudden ring of the door-bell. Those two, the phone and the doorbell, had a telepathic link ensuring the strident call of one was sufficient to set off the other in sympathetic response. This coincidental vying for attention as I endeavoured to answer both at the same time put such a strain on my diplomatic reserves it is little wonder I sometimes ended up satisfying neither the person at the door nor the caller on the line. And that was on a good day, when I wasn't caught in mid change, in a flurry of skirts, tops, knickers or what have you, in the mad dash to appear smart yet not miss the business on the doorstep. And the times I took long worrying reservations standing in the skimpiest of underwear when only one telephone served the household are legion, anxiously praying no one would demand attention at the door or wander into the kitchen where the telephone was placed.

'How do you stay so slim?' polite people ask, others put it differently, but I smile to myself thinking of all the adrenalin laden practice I had as a B&B wifie.

But then we got what I was sure would be the answer to all such problems, after I waded my way through the technicalities of setting up this wonderful piece of equipment, my brand new answerphone with its cordless handset! Magic!

And the technology worked, but it took a bit of a mind-set change for the value to kick in, my family still tending to demand an answer of my sweetly recorded statement of suggestion they call back later: *I'm sorry I can't take your call right now. Please leave a message, or call back later*, sounding good until, when playing back the tape, came the exasperated demand, 'Why, what's wrong with you?' followed by silence, then a fading irritated voice, 'I don't know what's wrong with that one today, saying to call her back later and never an explanation. I don't know what the world is...' crash! the rest lost as the receiver was banged down in disgust, usually by my mother who was not known within the family for keeping her angst to herself.

The real need for having an answerphone – prospective business – fared only marginally better in those early days of trial and error. The majority of my customers gasped their disbelief as they were met with a machine after several fruitless attempts to have their urgent and repetitive 'Hello!' replied to. This was followed by an exclamation of dissatisfaction to their other half, 'It's one of those dreadful machines again,' and down would go the receiver. This of course, was before the invention of mobile phones, inexpensive enough and neat enough to carry about without risking a double hernia.

The day of the camel caught me en route to the door, this time with all my clothes intact and the latest invention of mobility, popularly known as the-carry-about-phone, glued to my ear. This was a call I had no intention of losing, despite the difficult line. I had tried for ages to contact this company and my heart soared when at last a call back came, until the door-bell reminded the phone it was keeping to its end of the bargain.

Pulling open the door I plastered a big smile of welcome upon my face, at the same time asking the company caller, 'Could you hold the line a moment please.' On the doorstep were two crisp looking elderly ladies who meant business. The sterner of the two asked if we had a twin room, which we had, so I indicated they come into the hallway and pointed towards the lounge, ready to mouth, 'I'll be with you in a minute,' when the impatient caller crackled into my ear, 'This is a very bad line. I'll call you back later.'

'No! Please! Don't do that.' Panic overwhelmed me. I just about forgot the one woman still in the vestibule while the other came into the hall. 'This is urgent. I need to talk about the camel...'

She cut in quickly – she had obviously got my irate messages left over a period of several days. 'I can assure you, Mrs Campbell, a pair was sent!

'But I keep trying to tell you, I never got the other camel...' listening intently, desperate not to lose the call or the women looking for a room, I gave a tight smile.

'We have no more in stock. We can send an alternative...' crackled down the line.

I quickly interrupted, 'No! It has to be the camel. I already have the one camel and it's exactly what I want, but I need two.' More crackling followed as the two ladies, standing by, began to glance at each other, the crispness fading into puzzled concern.

'Look,' I replied, 'I sent for two camels. One arrived...yes, yes, in perfect condition...yes, it's the right size, but I need two and they have to match...no, that won't do. Can't you get another camel to match the one I have?' I listened while one lady edged towards the door, indicating to her friend to follow suit, but the friend was wide-eyed and listening.

Exasperated with the bad line and the lack of understanding on the other end, I implored. 'It's for the twins, so I need two camels of the same size. They've *got* to be the same colour. Can't you understand. I don't want a cream one, thank you.'

By now one of my seekers of sensible beds for the night was heading out the door, an urgent whispering going on between them. I picked up snatches of, 'Don't be ridiculous!' followed by '...what about all the llamas we passed coming here?' answered by, 'Llamas are one thing, camels are quite another!'

'I want to see this camel,' insisted the wide-eyed one with emphatic expectation.

By now I was torn between hearing more from the woman who was standing in front of me, her excitement exuding in equal measure to her friend's apprehension, and my caller on the hissing line implying if one component of the order arrived safely, then the other must have arrived too as they were dispatched together, by the same freight company. I had to defend my integrity.

'If you sent both then I can assure you, one went walk-about en route because only one arrived here. Now, are you going to send me the other one or do I have to send back the one I have and all the trouble that entails. You obviously don't appreciate the difficulties of transport in this remote area! I did pay for two and I do need them to be identical.'

My patience evaporated just as my would-be guest grabbed her gullible friend and dragged her away to a safer camel-free haven for the night. 'No thank-you!' I responded to another unsuitable offer. 'I really wanted two acrylic camels, advertised as a pair in your catalogue. I like the one I got but you can have it back!' and terminated the conversation, rushing out the door, but by now the car was speeding down the driveway, the exhaust a smoking two fingers to my offer of bed and breakfast, with or without a camel, or two!

Surely to goodness, despite passing the llama farm – at that time a wonder in the area – they didn't really believe I was stocking up on camels. Mind you, the Department of Agriculture was keen on any kind of diversification to sustain small bed and breakfast outlets. I doubt they would grant-aid camels, though the Highlands & Islands Development Board might have, such was their reputation to support the feeble-minded in their madcap schemes. They had been well known for their entrepreneurial encouragement into all sorts of ventures, but they preferred to grant-aid people to come into the areas to undertake those kinds of japes, not support natives like myself who should know better.

It was too funny to be annoyed at losing the custom, nevertheless, the episode did not end there. I eventually got my second acrylic camel, still have them, stored neatly in their requisite covers, each one labelled One Acrylic Camel, in a cupboard in the twin room so those who prefer a blanket to a duvet on their beds have the option.

Engrossed, a few nights later, in cooking dinner for a busy household, a voice of doom echoed from the kitchen table. 'The horses won't like it.'

I glanced at Neil, my young son, who was, unusually for him, tossing his food round his plate instead of its usual quick passage into his bottomless pit of a stomach. 'Won't like what?'

'When the llamas come.'

'Llamas? What llamas?

'The llamas you never said you were getting.'

'I'm not getting llamas. Are you mad?'

'Yes, you are. I heard it at school. And yes, I'm mad because I don't want llamas. The boys are all laughing about it and the girls say they can't wait 'til the llamas come.'

Now where did the two ladies spend the night I wondered, as I quietly smiled to myself. Wherever it was, the proprietors must have thought, Camels? Never! No, it must be llamas. After all, that female was the first person to take horses back into the village, long after the last Clydesdale disappeared, there no longer being work for horses and whoever heard of keeping horses just to play with! Oh, yes, it will be llamas next, mark my words! I could just hear them. So, now we were getting llamas, whether I and the horses liked it or not! I awaited further news of their impending arrival with tremendous interest.

There was enough trouble with the horses in those days and in more recent times, the new addition of one psychologically damaged cat gave cause for debate as to whether an animal-free home may have been the better option.

Take for instance, just after this final season opened, with one couple arriving and one leaving, I felt I had time to take on an extra chore.

'Did you do them?'

'Phew! Did it at last!' Grinning in heart-felt relief, I told the man Himself when he ventured back to the house for a coffee, reasoning that by now some form of normality would be found.

Rising euphoria at the sheer excitement of mission accomplished was a little dented when I surveyed the chaos of the kitchen. Coped vase of flowers, not broken though, water dripping everywhere, my one precious basil plant spewing earth all over the sink while bits of leaves remained stuck to the curtains. The vase of flowers had been a gift from the guests, rather beautiful lilies. Bet the pollen would never come out of the window blind, new only last year. Rubber glove ripped, first aid box tipped, by me in urgent scrabble for a couple of plasters and some disinfectant before everything got covered in blood. Large towel abandoned in the middle of the floor. Vegetable rack and contents scattered all over the floor. Blood-spattered dishcloth on work-top, my blood, not the cat's. Cat hair everywhere, some still floating gently to the floor to amass with the clusters of white fur swirling lazily in the gust of air as Himself closed the back door nervously.

'What's this then?' He looked at me with no sense of the bomb-shell he was dropping when he picked up a soggy white pill from the floor and held it aloft.

The heart went out of me.

It had been too good to be true, thinking I had wormed three cats in the space of two hours. It usually took three weeks, and that after spending a good ten days wondering, do I really need to do this.

Last time I did the dirty deed, the sudden capitulation of The Hobbit had me buoyed up thinking I could get maybe two cats done before guests arrived in the afternoon. The Hobbit is our boy cat, the biggest of the tribe, sporting alarmingly long talons, yet the best natured, not known for spitting, clawing or kicking. He could stop you in your tracks, at 20 paces, with a look that saw the grandchildren back off slowly and I rethinking any ill intent. The look was never converted into action. Probably because the fierceness of its delivery prohibited any further advancement towards him by anyone, especially me.

So, when it came to Hobby's turn for the pill, you sneaked up behind him so he couldn't warn you off with the look. It just took guts to do it and once you had him captured you had to carry it through, allowing him to know there was a purpose to what he saw as a vicious assault, so he wouldn't go for you because you sneaked up on him and grabbed him by the back of the neck for no good reason, his mother deploying such antics frequently. Then, last time, having psyched myself up for a week, and well prepared for a reasonable battle, I sidled up behind and grabbed him by the scruff. He eyed what he previously construed as the instrument of torture with a bored look, opened his mouth wide and made a big swallow; tablet gone! Then he looked at me with 'What's with the big deal?' written all over his beautiful striped face. I spent a good half hour looking for the pill, convinced he had tricked me, but no, the job had been done. What a fine cat.

You always did Hobby first anyway because, despite the look, he never went into an hysterical cacophony of warning screams like his sister, or viciously spat and hissed like his mother, putting you into a state of abject terror, rendering you incapable of tackling another cat for at least a week. The ideal is to have them all wormed as close in time as possible, but it seldom works out that way, so why I should think I had achieved the impossible that day, I don't know.

It can't just be me or our tribe of felines. Tell me of one person who does not have a problem worming a cat! Why don't the people who make things happen, generally known as 'they', *do* something about it?

A moan to the vet got sceptical looks, a procedural lecture and a small injection type tube which is certainly a step better than inserting the pill in the end of a straw and blowing down the cat's throat, suggested by someone who did not know our cats. I was desperate enough to try, forgetting that despite all provocation you do not suddenly inhale, not if you don't require worming yourself.

'I got wormed this morning,' does not go down particularly well with your guests, politely enquiring after your health as they innocently make their way in for breakfast. This unappreciated attempt at humour to deflect from the war wounds has an alarming effect. 'Worms? Worms!

Does she mean worms! She can't mean actual worms! Fleas! We were warned fleas were on the increase in certain accommodations, but a five star with worms?'

Even with the injection tube instead of the straw as your assistant, it's a totally dangerous operation. I've also tried following what I was assured are the fail-me-never guidelines from the vet of grabbing the cat by the back of the neck, lifting it, thus forcing open its jaws, and deftly injecting the tablet down the cat's throat with the tube placed over the cat's tongue. This has been known to achieve its objective inside an hour from first catching your cat, which is excellent progress.

The speed with which the cat uses its projectile abilities to shoot the pill back at you into the nether regions of the kitchen, never to be seen again, is progress in reverse. Despite your blood-spattered determination to keep clutching the cat, you must release the creature in order to get a new pill. So I've learned never ever to worm the cat with only one tablet in the pack, which means the starting point is usually the full set of nine tablets – yes, by now we have three cats, and they don't come cheap, nor do the pills.

The sudden burst of confidence that morning, after a week thinking about it, came when I saw The Hobbit sleeping comfortably in his hammock, the mother, Smudge, snaffle Poodie-Pooh's favourite basket in the window, and Poodie-Pooh, nicely cosseted in the boiler bed, sacrosanct territory of her mother's. This is par for the course and normal feline behaviour to set the seal upon the day. They all looked rather small and harmless and led me to announce boldly, 'Don't let any of the tribe out today. I'm going to do them.'

Now we were three hours down the line with confidence evaporating and panic encroaching as the clock ticked on and a room had to be prepared for the new arrivals. Note for the future: try and do the spring and autumn wormings before arrival and after departure of all paying guests.

Seeing my crestfallen face at the sight of the soggy pill in his hand, Himself, ever the gentleman, offered, 'I'll give you a hand. Then you can help me with the garden. What stage are you at?' He had never involved himself before and I wondered at the wisdom, but sighed thankfully; it was a buyers market. I speculated on the cost, but only for a moment. I was desperate enough to dismiss my natural disinclination to all things bargained for with Himself and all things wet and cold in a garden, but I threw caution to the wind and thanked him profusely.

Resisting the temptation to have a reviving brandy, I opted for strong coffee laced with thick double cream and explained, 'Hobby just opened his mouth and took his medicine like a man. Then, just like a man, he took off round the kitchen, doing a lap of honour, which, of course, put the others on full alert.'

'So it had to be Smudge next. Despite her protestations and scene-making abilities, you know she's easier to cope with than Pooh. It wasn't easy though! You know how Hobbit likes to wind his mother up. Well, he sure had her going, up and practising her spitting technique, crawling into every distant corner. But I got her and I did her, so that's two done.' I genuinely needed all my courage to tackle Poodie-Pooh, but now she was nowhere to be seen. 'Anyway, you must have let Pooh out, so what's the point. Why have we got cats instead of a loveable, obedient, happy to please, pill-eating dog?' I philosophised.

'I never let Pooh out. Look!' He pointed to the top of the cupboards. At first I saw nothing, then a pair of large yellow-green eyes blinked at me from the furthermost recesses of a dark corner. How would I get her down from there! Hobby often perked up his afternoons with gigantic leaps to the top of the wall cupboards but I had never seen Pooh up there before. Hobby, having dangerously long legs with springs attached, came down of his own accord. Pooh was not likely to, not today anyway.

'I've started, so I'll finish,' I announced, in true Mastermind fashion. The coffee, or maybe it was the cream, bolstered my resolve.

'Is Smudge all right? Did you do her okay?' the concern in his voice was obviously for the cat so I answered irritably, waving my bandaged hand in the air, 'You never 'do' Smudge okay but I did her, eventually. She wasn't exactly pleased and I got a good solid spitting and one big scratch before she demanded out the window to glare at me from outside. You would think they could invent something to prevent all this cruelty and distress to people!' I felt a trickle of sweat run down my back at the prospect of tackling Pooh again. The spat out pill was the one I had been foolish enough to think I had got down her reluctant throat.

'Right, I'll get Pooh now.' Bold words as I added a step-ladder to the chaos. 'Get the towel. She'll need to be wrapped securely in it first.'

'Don't be silly,' said Himself pulling on large leather gauntlets last seen shovelling coal into the shed, the boiler suit he was already encased in for his outside work appeared suitable apparel for the job.

Pooh is not a big cat, but she's well rounded because she eats her kills after presenting them for inspection, though weasels are for display purposes only. You're given about two seconds to make up your mind if you want this gift she would much rather keep for herself, but feline protocol demands she offer it first. Other than her hideous behaviour at worming time, Pooh is the best mannered of cats. A very fine cat indeed, and a ferocious hunter to boot. She's just as ferocious an eater, always checking her mother's and brother's dishes to see no favouritism destroys harmony, unless to her advantage. She's also a steadfast defender of her space when it comes to human interference bordering on the unwanted. Hobby is different. He doesn't give a stuff about food and allows an in-depth testing of his meals by the diligent Pooh to make sure all is well. She's a very caring cat and possessively loving to Himself and myself but with little time for anyone else. She views our son and his family with suspicion and candid dislike.

They come in, she goes out.

She is also very unforgiving. At only a few months old she took it into her head to go on a long safari, turning up nine months later to a hero's welcome from her brother, long after we had mourned her death. Two months on, when Hobby took a short holiday in the hills, aided and abetted by his mother who was convinced she could get rid of him, Pooh's mournful howls and complete refusal to eat for the first week of his absence caused as much distress to us as The Hobbit's sudden loss. After ten days I put a notice of his disappearance in the local shop, describing his apparel at time of going: brown striped waistcoat with matching hat and long white breaches, indeed, his Sunday best. A phone call alerted me to seek him in an area known for its wildlife, but despite my anxious search and much calling there was no sign of him. Next morning, Himself gleefully egged me to visit the 'shed' beloved of those happy days when Connie worked with us, making certain the animals were as well looked after as the humans. There was The Hobbit, sleeping peacefully in one of their many outdoor beds. Was Pooh pleased? Not a bit of her. He was severely reprimanded and for four long weeks she adamantly refused to acknowledge him, demanding all her meals be taken outside.

He came in, she went out.

He went out. She came in. It was a dreadfully difficult time as she played out her offended feelings to best purpose. She refused to share with him either the garage with its cat-flap and choice of beds, or the greenhouse. This all three had commandeered as an outside cat-house, handy for entertaining 'the Boyfriend', in reality Hobby's childhood pal and the only cat allowed on the premises, but fought over by Smudge and Pooh, each insisting he was *her* boyfriend.

'The Boyfriend's back,' we would tell each other and wonder how much skin and hair would fly today while Hobby and his large black tomcat friend quietly sat on walls chewing over old times. The Boyfriend always seemed to have a smirk on his coal-black face.

Smudge viewed all this angst against Hobby's return without prejudice, firmly swiping out at both of them as was her custom. She changed her mind about keeping them ten days after the decision was made that, having harassed so many innocent people for stealing two of her kittens when successfully homed, we could not possibly deprive her of the other two. By the time she would cunningly entice them outside just to inflict a hefty swipe upon their innocent heads, they were part of our family. We felt sure she was merely going through a disciplinary phase bringing up her children in a manner the human race is now warned against in our nanny state, infused with politically correct advice to keep our mitts to ourselves and let our offspring rule the roost. Judging the standard of behaviour from the two kittens as they grew up, excepting the worming shenanigans, I think the cat had it sussed.

Smudge was, however, paranoid: we conceded to that, discovering her condition not too long after signing the adoption papers that saw her wave goodbye to her SSPCA shelter and at ten weeks old, proceed to close down my business due to irrational behaviour involving the guests, upsetting veterinary staff while hospitalised, and generally causing mayhem wherever she went. She insisted upon accompanying me on trips, whether a day shopping or overnight, or just to the local shop, attracting unbelievable attention in hotels and car parks alike. She looks deceptively sweet with her gleaming black and white coat, black cap extending to just beneath her almond green eyes, white mask with that big black smudge on her nose, and hind legs too long to balance her gait as she lopes off like a startled hare. She is, nevertheless, an excellent hunter, and that being her modus operandi, she came to stay.

Mind you, there was a period of time when a card was displayed in the vet's, on her behalf, seeking a new home. She came to us courtesy of a previous girlfriend of Neil's and was king of the castle as no other creature, two-legged or four, was now in our household to compete for attention. The horses were gone, the rabbits were gone, Felix, at 21 years succumbed to old age and was interned, with unbelievable sadness, under a Caithness flagstone in the back garden. Notices of her death were sent to all her favourite guests with the intimation we would not be getting another cat. Not long after Smudge's unexpected arrival, Anne and Neil's relationship ended and as Anne was returning to University, Smudge became our cat. I have no doubt she missed Anne's loving care and played us up at every opportunity.

Our spoiled and extremely naughty young cat would have been about a year old when Neil first introduced his new friend Katrina into our household and that didn't go down too well either. His punishment was piddle in any bag of belongings he left lying open when rushing to and from the oil rigs where he now worked. A year of outrageous behaviour followed after which the traumatic birth of her own four kittens got the desired 'oh, what a clever cat am I' effect but when this was followed very shortly by the birth of our first grandchild, she saw nothing clever about it and took tremendous exception to this attention-seeking, smelly, bundle. She soon sussed out where to lay blame for usurping her kittens and took it out on Katrina and 'her kitten' at every opportunity.

After being an exemplary mother she made it very clear she thought all kittens, especially of the human kind, should be re-homed by the age of 16 weeks and the fact we did nothing about it led to tremendous bouts of wickedness. We carefully watched her glowering stares and orchestrated avoidance of the baby, accepting her dislike of this unpredictable little creature who squealed loudly and drew attention from her. As Shane became an unsteady toddler, she took to luring the growing child with enticingly waving tail, little friendly purrups and backward glances to follow her, out of sight of adults where she would soundly administer a hefty cuff, exactly as she did to the kittens, never drawing blood, just terrorising them all in equal measure.

Then one night, before Neil was due to return to his rig she did the unthinkable and lashed out at the child as he passed her at eye-level. She drew blood. The child was scratched, not badly, but enough to earn a horrified reaction. The cat, who had never caused quite such a furore before, seemed as truly shocked as the rest of us.

'Have her out of here before I get back, or *I'll* get rid of her,' was the distraught father's demand. Katrina and I were devastated. We had words with the cat, we had words with the child, who had never laid a finger on her. He was one year old and deeply upset. Himself had strong words for all of us and I had very serious words with myself feeling totally responsible for the incident.

We had to show willing to relocate the cat so we spoke to the vet and a card was written up for display at appropriate points. Despite the miscreant's utter contempt for Katrina, Shane's patient mother, the wayward cat had an ally in her. Words which were supposed to have found her a new home in a child- and kitten-free environment became, *'Black and white female cat. Hates children. Bites old ladies. Good hunter. Health problems, difficult and expensive to treat. Must go to active home as partial to long walks showing painful – for owner – withdrawal symptoms if specific needs not met. Smudge well used to visiting vet. Has feisty hatred for vets. Likes shopping and picnic lunches, best ham and chicken preferred, in company, yours preferably, so owner must have time to give her. Has problem believing she is a cat. After several warnings, must vacate warm, loving, home, no longer able to tolerate her devious behaviour.'* The heading was *Desperately Seeking Smudge!*

'Any response to the card?' Neil would ask when he phoned Katrina, not knowing the card's content. 'No,' she would sigh, 'Can't understand no one wanting a good young hunting cat like Smudge.'

'Did you put a photo of her on it?' His determined query had Katrina think quickly. 'No, she wouldn't stay still for a picture,' whereas the truth was, a snap of the beautiful creature could have tempted someone into taking her.

By the time Neil returned we were convinced Smudge had learned a lesson and though we had laid it on thick, knowing none would respond, sadly, the card was closer to the truth than a character assassination. Who else would have her, and despite her attitude problem, we all, including Shane and Neil, loved her. So no more was said, and never again did she touch a child, but to this day, a wary eye is kept on her when children are about. Apart from a tendency to bite old ladies in her first year, she astounds us by being particularly friendly to guests, especially men, allowing fur to be ruffled that would earn us a good cuffing.

Shane, a genuine animal lover, sighs, 'I never ever touched her,' and makes up for his distrust of her with a reciprocal love of Hobby who would go off out on the fields to watch over the small child at play and remains a steadfast friend to the now ten year old boy. Pooh studiously dislikes them all, and Hobbit proved his individuality by taking an immediate and intense dislike to their second child, Fallon. He does not leave the house when she arrives but makes his feelings known with the look. She never turns her back on him, sidling past, and even Shane nervously backs off at times, shouting, 'Granny, The Hobbit is looking at me!' Yet, Fallon likes nothing better than stories that include all the cats, especially Pooh. She admires the cats' abilities to appear to do as they please, convinced the 'kittens' attend school in the hills every week day, Pooh managing to upset Teacher-Cat every day by being late, no matter how early she gets up or sets off on each adventurous journey.

Causing mayhem and demanding walks or rides in the car appeared to be Smudge's raisons d'etre, and being hyperactive, we wondered how to calm her down. Against veterinary advice I must admit, we let her have those kittens thinking that will settle her. Apart from the peculiarity of insisting I stand mid-wife for the birth of all four kittens, she proved an exemplary mother and we have video footage of her persistence in ensuring all her brood learn to enjoy long walks, as she did, climb trees, as she did, hunt to her satisfaction and be meticulously clean. She also taught them many other idiosyncrasies, so her kittens could be identified by some highly suspect behaviour long after being homed. It did my reputation no good at all.

The tales of their odd, highly amusing, and at times almost human behaviour are too numerous to tell, and the strength of each character keeps you as much on your toes as any inspector. Pooh, the one about to be wormed, though the most affectionate, seldom forgets an insult, finding ways of making you pay for any inferred offence.

When we take a holiday, Neil and Katrina, living close by, feed and generally ensure the tribe are looked after during our absence. The cats accept this double-barrelled insult with various reactions. Going away is bad enough but leaving us with *them?* What are you thinking of, they yowl and prowl around us the moment they spy a suitcase or travel bag bigger than my overnight, which they check out but accept without too much fuss. She's off skiving again, they agree, commiserating with Skimbleshanks as they ensure he puts their needs before his own.

Last time we returned from a five-week safari to Africa, Pooh had gone missing. Nothing new here. It once took us two weeks to find Smudge and another two weeks of persuasion to get her back home. Apparently her then boyfriend, the father of her kittens, a handsomely striped stray tom known to us as The Daddy Cat, took her to the large garden belonging to the family who fed him. They were bird lovers and encouraged this lovely, though feral, tomcat because he did not chase birds, nor did the little black and white cat he often turned up with, so when she arrived as his constant companion, they fed her too. As ever, she found other ways of blotting her copy-book and eventually a notice was posted in the local shop – how we traced her – pleading with the owners of the cat with the black smudge on its nose, to please rescue them from her ever increasing demands. Their teenage children wanted the cat in the house, despite their allergies. Their large barking dog wanted the cat in the house too, so he could kill her. We were shocked to hear the cat began importuning at the windows; she had insisted to us that she loathed dogs, was very frightened of them, and we must never allow guests to bring dogs into the house. She could not bear to be anywhere near dogs, emphatically drumming this into us until I ended up turning away lucrative dog-loving trade, just to please her. She was very strict about this rule and taught her kittens to hate dogs too. And now she wanted to stay with a dog. Enticed into her favourite mode of transport, my car, I eventually persuaded her to spend the better part of her time at home, so these kind people could be left in peace with their stray tom.

Shortly afterwards, we noticed a decline in Smudge and it was only when discovering The Daddy Cat had been killed on the road, we remembered a similar decline as a young cat, when Big Tom, the first big love of her life, had been found dead in a neighbour's outhouse. The Boyfriend, too, came to a much mourned end, so Smudge suffered for her love affairs, but is never without a boyfriend, and that her daughter should demand a share of her admirers was a positive outrage!

Sitting in my office upon that last return home from holiday four years ago, I heard the racing footsteps of six-year-old Shane as he thundered towards the back door. 'They said I wasn't to tell you!' came his panting goggle-eyed greeting. 'What's happened,' my voice rose a decibel or two in anxiety, 'and why am I not to be told?'

'It's soooo bad,' he gasped, staring intently at me, 'and Dad was using the F-word...a lot.'

I flew out the door prepared for anything but by now his parents had arrived with Pooh in a box, found in a snare with her throat cut.

Katrina was heavily pregnant with Fallon and had been unable to stop Shane racing ahead of them with his sorry tale. Pooh was very badly cut. Persuading her out of the rabbit burrow, carrying her back to their garage and cutting the wire had been a nightmare experience with her natural, or maybe unnatural, dislike of them heightened into a spitting, snarling fury. Whisked in to the vet, she stayed there for a long anxious 24 hours. Next day I ferried her home, very sorry for herself, to be greeted by howls of laughter from Shane. 'She looks just like ET,' he kept saying!

Whether it was their laughing at her long shaven neck, or being the ones responsible for her when she got caught in the snare, then putting her through hell cutting her free, that caused her forever afterwards to take one startled look at them with 'They're the ones who cut my throat and you're letting them into the house?' writ large on her face, that began her complete avoidance of my little family. So, when they come in, she goes out, an arrangement still in place today.

This does not make life easy as our family spend a lot of time here, a time we all enjoy, the welcome ever-ready, except from her, and her mother who likes to take the side of adversity and has no time for soppy peacemakers.

Eventually, with the help of Himself, the gauntlets and the towel he initially discarded as superfluous, we wormed her. Job done, she created merry hell over the state of her normally gleaming white coat. Now she was a dirty shade of grey with heavy black fingerprints, here, there and everywhere, compliments of the gauntlets. Not a pretty sight, and no doubt another unforgivable dereliction of duty. She knew she had to be done, but in her eyes, I had once again made a poor fist of things and would be at the receiving end of much feline disdain before we settled down to normal relations. Until the next time.

Does anyone, other than a fully trained vet, actually know how to worm a cat?

7

Sabotaged By British Telecom

I OPENED THE DOOR to a cheerful greeting of 'Hello! We reserved a room, a week ago,' from a middle-aged couple on the doorstep. When fully booked, I tried to memorise the three sets of names, usually a couple allocated to each room we now had on offer, so that when I went to the door, none of the antics of the past resurfaced; stuffing people into the wrong rooms, sometimes with the wrong partners, to their great confusion. Not to be encouraged since becoming a rather sedate five star establishment and me with sufficient grey hairs not to get off with such giddy behaviour, brought on, in the main, by the belief a pre-dinner G&T would settle me nicely into the long night of work ahead.

I always did have a generous hand when dishing out anything to be consumed, my measurements certainly not regulated by how many nips could be got out of a bottle. Much better fun seeing how many nips could be got into a glass and still keep control of the job. It was the control factor that let me down.

After a couple of entanglements with people backing out of rooms on being met by a complete stranger sitting on the bed, or a lascivious eye cast on the wrong husband or wife because I insisted that, yes, that was their room, little noticing it was not the correct person I was encouraging into its depths. After downing a large gin and tonic, you would be surprised at the uniformity of size and colouring in individuals who booked in at exactly the same time. The problem only arose when arrivals chose to congregate en masse on the doorstep, or within minutes of each other, then rush back and fore with luggage, meeting me in the hallway, innocently asking, 'Is that my room?' Similarities in looks, especially if Italian, completely threw me. 'Yes,' I would glibly answer, then had to tear back to sort it out when I heard a gasped apology from some poor innocent soul when he staggered in, bags in hand, to be met by an indignant stranger!

So my only opportunity to enjoy a relaxing drink, that G&T before finalising dinner preparations, had to go by the board, there being no time whatsoever after that for any such indulgences. Finishing time was always well past midnight and with an early start essential, I had to have a clear head to greet the birds as they belted out their dawn chorus.

This pre-dinner drinks date had been a great little ritual and looked forward to with childish delight, when Himself appeared all spruced up after a mucky day on the croft. It only happened when he was at home – when he was not, the idea of drinking a G&T on my own would have seemed alien. It was the only time in a long hard working day when we could sit and catch up on the happenings in each other's corners of power. As I began to cook, happily chatting, within reach of a charged glass, I little thought this style of food preparation would hold a fascination for the general public, to be enacted on TV screens across the country when chefs encouraged such practice with a glass decidedly more half full than half empty. My mistake had been substituting gin for wine and not appreciating the difference in alcohol content, never mind in quantity, being then unaware of the delights that awaited me as I learned to emulate those TV chefs with their glass of wine on the side.

After admiring the beautifully set table, confident all food was fully prepped, I would wait for new arrivals, many cutting it as close to dinner time as possible, all too often appearing in one great rush. A natural curiosity as to the nature of our newcomers turned to anxiety the later they chose to arrive. We dealt with five different rooms then, so invariably there would be late-comers, little knowing the excitement on offer when I exceeded their expectations in a manner not advocated by the tourism advisors! After trying to entice them into spending the night with a complete stranger once too often, I made the sensible switch to the T, leaving out the G, after which all went well, except it wasn't near such fun – for any of us!

I was caught out trying to stuff the wrong person into a room on one occasion when nothing more potent than water passed my lips. It was a dreadful day of pouring rain, Neil was home on leave from the Marines, Himself out on the croft exercising his right to boss his son about and I was preparing dinner for four forestry chaps who had yet to arrive. When the doorbell rang I found four very tall lads, kitted out in their forest greens, some with head protection, all standing on the front step in a torrential downpour.

'Oh, do come in out of the rain and never mind that,' I implored as the first chap stopped to take off his boots, noticing they were an extremely handsome bunch, especially the first young man over the door as he went into the hall shaking water from his drenched cap. I closed the door indicating that two should go upstairs to the twin, and two down the corridor to the other twin, and followed the first two, opening the bedroom door. 'That's one room there. Is that all right for you?' I politely asked the young man who had come in first, anxious to show them the upstairs room so they could sort themselves out and get off their dripping gear.

'Mother!'

I spun round and looked at my so-called forester properly for the first time and felt such a fool. His disbelief didn't help as the others looked askance, doubt creeping into their anticipation that they were booked into a decent place. They'd all looked pretty much alike to me, handsome virile young men. How was I to know my son would be ushering them in. I hardly saw him nowadays, anyway, and where was the fourth fellow, confusing me like that! He arrived, staggering under bags, to find his colleagues in fits of laughter and Neil trying to explain his dipsy – but most certainly not tipsy – mother's behaviour!

On this much more recent occasion I could have done with a measure of Dutch Gin courage to get me out of the tangle I was in and it was all down to the wonderful service British Telecom afford their loyal customers. Every page of their spiel, be it on the internet, or in their directory, or the enticing letters to lure people into purchasing their product from BT, told me of their outstanding customer care. To whom they delivered this praiseworthy service is a mystery because it certainly was not to me, a lifelong customer, with all telecommunications bought through their good selves. Even my mobile was theirs, for goodness sakes!

I put my woes to one side as I introduced myself with a wide smile and asked their name. 'The Manns,' was said with smiling expectation.

'Manns?' my smile faded. We had the Basstoes already staying, the Strimers and the MacLeods arriving, but no Manns. It's a heart stopping moment and requires steely resolve to keep the head followed by an assuring invitation to come into the lounge, sit down calmly and we will soon get to the bottom of what has happened, all the time accepting blame, even when you know different, constantly saying we shall sort it out. Shades, actually, of the BT call centre at their expressive best, insisting they will sort out the problem, except we in the private sector must fix our problems, as and when they happen. Imagine if I pointed to a chair in the lounge and told my guest, 'Sit there for 48 hours and I'll get back to you when I can!' I discovered British Telecom to be very keen on the 48 hour opt out clause when problems arose.

Bookings made under the name of one partner from a couple who then give the other's name upon arrival can cause consternation, but are quickly resolved. Bookings made by an agency where you have the agency name in the register rather than the client's cause similar reaction but again are easily fixed and smiles resurface quickly. Bookings made at another establishment while the guests in your lounge insist they are booked with you takes a bit of detective work, and much swallowing, from you, of their attitude, but they too get sorted, and if you're lucky, you get an abject apology from an embarrassed couple when you source their proper destination, or, as has happened, a right tantrum. 'But that's not where I meant to book in. It was with you and you do have a room!'

Never, in all my years have I ever taken a booking that belonged elsewhere, preferring an empty room to that kind of conniving. Yet, in the early days I was hit by this delightful 'what's yours is mine if I can get my hands on it first' way of doing business on more than one occasion, whilst I, poor mug, waited all evening with dinner half prepared and little sleep, wondering which hospital my guests could be in. Getting found out a couple of times put a stop to such practices, on one memorable occasion our local TIC officer was entangled into the deceit, which helped considerably to put a stop to such greed.

But this was different. I could feel it in my bones and as my face fell, theirs took on a grim look of: she's gone and cocked up our booking! Not me m'Lud I would love to have said, but instead felt obliged to take the rap for BT, the ratbags!

The origins of the problem arose one merry morning when, very early as is my habit, I attempted to catch up with my emails, having spent the previous day – after seeing to the needs of guests in the early morning – at a meeting in Inverness. Naturally, I shopped, but not in the abandoned card-carrying devil-may-care bout of retail therapeutic indulgence I would have liked. Instead diligently searching out the accoutrements of my trade I could not buy locally, stacking the BMW with its relatively spacious boot, to the gunwales, I got back too late to care what was waiting in my email in-box and knew I would be up with the lark and have a chance to start on the contents of both car and in-box early next day.

The early-morning smile was soon wiped off my face. I was blocked out, rejected, sent packing, a padlock I had never witnessed before with a message saying my password was unrecognisable to my mail server. I had not changed it or any other aspect of my package with Btyahoo.com, my service provider. As advised I tried to sort it out online but failed miserably. Such a lot of work to do after a day stocking up and always the following day would be a catching up exercise, this one being no exception. And I no longer had the steadfast resolve of Connie to assure, 'We'll sort it out, what we will!' How I missed her, realising at last that no matter how long I kept her job open for her, she was not going to come back. The pain she had suffered from, in her knee and back, almost from her first year with me, building up to such extent, she eventually moved from 'We'll see how it goes,' to the inevitable, 'You'll manage fine without me.' I managed, but I would never say fine, and it was not near such fun. Himself and myself could have great confabs, a deep friendship bonding the astrological differences of our diverse personalities that allowed us a marriage, if not made in heaven, then on pretty solid foundations. But, it was not the same fun without Connie, never the degeneration into howling laughter, most of the time at incidents put there to test our ability, not our humour. And then Himself never was half as capable as Connie when it came to trapping the feral cats, visiting the vet, or turning our many outings, when we pretended to be tourists, into care-free adventures that brooked no such demands as, 'Hell, we should be getting back!'

So I took the bull by the horns, with only Himself to get on with the real work as he said, and succumbed to what I knew would be a long session on a BT premier call number. I listened to all the electronic advice before hearing the heavily accented, by now familiar tones of our Indian friends who manned the call centre. I had, since going onto wireless broadband spent many an afternoon in India having one or other of my server's faults sorted. It took time, considerable time, but faults were always fixed, polite exchanges made and good-byes happily said. Forms of satisfaction were filled in to their credit and little annoyances forgotten in the relief to get the by now over-heated phone and their dreadful holding music away from my ears!

My last email had come in on 10 July and all had been well. But Thursday 12 July was a different kettle of fish. Coming up on two hours into the conversation, sprinkled with many 'Pardons' from my side and many, 'Do not worry, Madam, we are fixing the problem,' on their side, I finally persuaded the advisor to get someone else on the line. I then had had the frustration of watching him keying wrong user names and wrong passwords into wrong areas before correcting them during his access session on my computer. With frustration steaming up the office windows, this time the satisfaction sheet was filled in with growling dissatisfaction and a niggle of mounting anxiety. How could they not fix their own problem? The superior I demanded to speak with, to my abject horror, curtly informed me I would be contacted within 48 hours by someone who would have the problem fixed.

'Do not worry, Madam. We are fixing the problem,' became a sing-song mantra and little did I know just how familiar it was going to become.

A lengthy two day inactive email address to a business that takes its bookings in by internet, and sends dozens of emails to the agencies they work with, not forgetting I was in email communication with the publisher of my first book, *The Land Beyond The Green Fields*, with articles to get to editors as well – it was tantamount to laying the foundations to an almighty seizure!

As to the mainstay of our income, I vaguely tried to remember who all had been replied to by email with availability and what was their possibility of confirmation. You could not second guess that one. So I had to wait, a maximum of 48 hours they assured me, with response, so they said, more likely to be well within that time. What charming optimists these BT call centre employees are! With a final, 'Do not worry, Madam, we are fixing the problem,' I rested the receiver along with my brain, my eyes and my ears. My tongue had been little used in the two hour travail so I screamed my frustration at the walls giving the cats one hell of a fright.

Ah ha! Now they know how I feel when they do that.

The following day passed with no contact from these darling people at British Telecom.

I thought I would alleviate my anxiety by having a reassuring word with BT's Customer Care. Thirty minutes down the line, being assured by BT's automated response, they were *very* busy but they *would* answer my call proved too much for my fragile concerns that by now there was bound to be many enquiries and possible confirmations, so I slammed down the receiver, dived into the nearest bathroom and threw up. Looks of anxiety began to cross feline faces and Himself took off for the safer haven of mowing the lawns, with ear plugs in place.

The next day, exactly 48 hours after the promised call that never came, I once again tried to speak with anyone at BT but found the only people I could speak with were my friends at the call centre in India. At least they were actual people, not electronic Big Brother style voices, demanding I key in a variety of numerals that eventually led me back to the beginning of the menu.

Each time I accessed the call centre I was greeted as a new customer, with a new complaint, inferring they had only just known of it so could not understand my frustration. 'Control yourself,' one woman strongly advised when my voice rose a few decibels. This time, an hour into the call that failed to right the wrong, I had sufficient wit to ask for a reference number to go with the solemn promise that I would be called back in 24 hours. Seems ridiculous, but to me a bit of a victory, 24 being half the wait of 48. The reference number too would stop them treating each call as a new complaint which was time consuming and very frustrating. Having dealt out a number they said their polite goodbyes with great cheer, as if the number was key to solving my entire costly problem. By now I had empty rooms when they should have been full. Business had come to an ignominious halt.

Spurred on by staring at the blank spaces in the register, with reference number in hand, I had another go which got me exactly nowhere. With 'Do not worry, Madam, we are fixing the problem,' and the added insult of 'and thank you for choosing BT Total Broadband as your choice of server!' echoing in my ears, I growled loudly to no one in particular. Everyone was taking the cats' advice and staying well away from me.

In desperation I tried 'faults', but got an electronic voice that sounded very annoyed with me for wasting its time as it assured me it had tested the line I was speaking from and there was no fault on it! Suitably chastened, I waited anxiously for it to tell me to put down the receiver and control myself, but instead I was calmly offered the option of listening to the menu again. It had got over its little tantrum. I got over mine about ten minutes after downing a strong coffee laced with double cream, there being no brandy to hand. The cats, to their credit, were giving the house a bit of a wide berth.

I began talking to myself, saying, in sing-song mantra style, 'thank you for choosing BT Total Broadband as your choice of tormentors!'

Innocent people who did not know of the debacle destroying the last months of what I had hoped would be a lucrative lead into retirement after 40 years caring for other people, listened to my intense mutterings, looked at my white sleepless face and asked, 'Are you all right?'

'Oh, yes,' I would answer in a sing-song voice, 'My problems are being fixed and in 48 hours everything will be restored to normal.'

The following day, once again failing to get to speak to any at BT other than the Indian call centre, I argued my case with my reference number and was assured it was not a BT problem, which was news to me, good or bad I did not dare to ponder, but different at least.

'Is it my computer?' I tentatively enquired, but thought not as the guarantee was still in effect and these things usually got me the day after the guarantee ran out.

'No, Madam, we can assure you your computer is not at fault.'

'Have I a virus?' I queried.

'No, Madam, we can assure you, you have no virus.'

'Has somebody tried to hack into my files and knackered them then?'

Long pause. 'Pardon?'

It was usually I who made the polite pardons in these long-distance conversations.

'Is someone trying to bug me?' other than you, I longed to add but I had to control myself.

'No, Madam, we would know if there was any problem at your end.'

Relief, but if the problem were not theirs, and it was not mine, then who's, I queried between gritted teeth, was it?

'The problem belongs to Yahoo,' the lilting voice assured me.

'But you are Yahoo!'

'No, Madam, we are BT.'

'Listen,' I said, controlling myself, 'I signed up with BT many years ago. BT signed up with Yahoo to become partners in crime, so as far as I am concerned, you and Yahoo are one and the same company, delivering an expensive service to my home for which I pay. You are Btyahoo.com, are you not?'

'Oh, yes, Madam, we are Btyahoo.com you are speaking to.' The pride with which this was announced over the airways should have won my advisor a bonus. Had I been near him, it would have won him a boot up the backside!

'Well, are you going to get the problem fixed then?'

'No, Madam. We are unable to fix the problem because the problem is with Yahoo.'

I put down the phone and cried. The cats, with furtive backwards glances, all asked out, wondering which of them had done what this time.

Then a flash of inspiration. I rang back, went through all the paraphernalia of explanations then, after being told again that the problem was with Yahoo, I asked with baited breath. 'Can I speak with Yahoo, then?'

'If you will hold the line for two minutes, I will talk to my colleagues at Yahoo and see if I can connect you.'

Wow! Success, possibly, surely, or at least they can tell me what is actually wrong and why it is taking this inordinate length of time to put it right. What *is* this problem we keep referring to? I needed to know.

By now I had dozens of two minute holds under my belt which had always been nothing less than five minutes, listening to excruciatingly awful music. Not even Indian music, which I rather like after enjoying jaunting round many areas of that vast and fascinating county, long before British Telecom saw fit to use its people as a cheap source of labour for their call centres and then widen the area of discontent by joining up with Yahoo!

Five minutes grew to 15 with inevitable interruptions of, 'Thank you for your patience Madam,' to which a grunt of disgust was not accepted as a reply, nor was a disdainful silence, so I *had* to acknowledge each frustrating interruption which conveyed nothing other than the time-wasting statement they were still in contact with their colleagues. So, no matter how trivial the comment they came back online to make, such as a sudden 'thank you for your patience' whilst I was sitting in a lather of impatience, or a sudden, 'please do not worry, Madam', was repeated until I gave a recognisable and concise answer. I resisted the temptation to answer back at my most caustic, because I had to control myself.

I do hope I am not boring you because I am only half way through the saga to date and, with it still to be resolved, a new and highly alarming side-effect entered the arena; as if my incoming telephone calls developed a default mechanism each time I pick up the receiver to hear the peevish accusation, 'You never replied to my email,' clearly implying I am less than diligent, that phrase becoming as familiar as, 'Do not worry, Madam, we are fixing the problem.' So I added to my head-down mutterings, 'You never replied to my emails!' and have the satisfaction of hearing everyone else say an irritated, 'Pardon?'

As for India, they never called back despite profuse assurances but when I accessed them, my anxious 'Pardons?' were a thing of the past. I am now so familiar with the musical intonations and delightful cadences of their speech, I can fully understand the many questions and instructions rattled off between five and 15 minute bursts of music, a cacophony that would never grow on me.

I spent a sleepless night that evening, visions of padlocks filtering past my eyes in horrid flashbacks as my brain kept revisiting my email of its own accord. Eventually I fell into a fitful sleep to find myself distressed at being locked *out* of the Tower of London while blackbirds stuck their heads out of pies and in sing-song voices kept telling me not to worry, they would fix the problem and let me in.

Bleary eyed next day, I followed my sister's advice and rang BT in the late afternoon making several valiant attempts to get a real person on the line. Sandra had only just survived her own daily encounter with my Indian friends, whom she had great difficulty in persuading that her problem was a telephone that made no ringing sound, therefore she was missing all her incoming calls. Each time they patiently told her to put down her receiver, Madam, and they would ring her back later, after they did a check! Her hysterical queries of, 'And how am I going to know the phone is ringing when it cannot ring?' was firmly and politely ignored. She, however, was never told to control herself during several calls she made over several days in an attempt to sort it all out.

At another time I would have laughed.

Her daughter told her to try again at a certain time and she would get a UK-based engineer, which she did, and the problem was identified easily and soon sorted by that person saying, 'Pick up the phone in exactly five minutes and I will be on the line.'

How sensible. Being the eternal optimist, I had visions of getting my problem sorted by finding this person at the appropriate time. I tried mid-afternoon but it was late afternoon before the constant recording telling me that they *would* answer my call proved fruitful, and I got a person. A short-lived triumph though. Another foreign person, with that familiar sing-song accent, and particularly difficult to understand, my sob story meeting with a curt transfer to the Indian call centre, insisting only they could help me. 'Like they have for the past week?' That brought no understanding or sympathy, narrowly missing a warning to control myself.

Back to square one except now I was fluent in both language and instruction and lightening quick with all my responses and actions in transferring the pc to their tender mercies across the continents. They had, during previous transfers, got rid of my passwords and keyed in their own, on several occasions so now I wasn't sure if I was *welcome1, internet2, joan11, or london10,* as I tried to keep track of it all. I tried to inject some humour with an enthusiastic shout of, 'Give me *Scottishwifie1*' but that threw so many, 'Pardons?' into the pot, I gave up. Losing the head completely, I slammed down the receiver, jumped up and down and screamed, 'If I can pardon you lot, it will be a miracle.' The cats took off, en masse.

One day, though, I thought I should try keying in a new password of my own to see if that would help, and felt I should tell them. When I offered them my password so they knew how to access my account while they were fixing the problem, they, having issued me with a variety of different passwords over the previous week, gave me a sound ticking off, 'Do not give me your password Madam. That is confidential.' I gave him my reference number and waited about 20 minutes for him to become conversant with the problem, to consult with his colleagues, and asked him again if he wanted the new password. 'No, Madam,' I was very firmly told. He then proceeded to change the password, and naturally, told me what it was. I'm not quite sure of the technical difference between him telling me, or me telling him, but there you go! Another BT, or is it a Yahoo, puzzle.

I am now getting confused myself, though all past confusions over the last 10 years I have blamed on Scottish Water. I'm convinced they're putting something into the supply that keeps us questioning our memories. They could be in cahoots with the government on a project of 'de-familiarisation' so we forget what dire attacks they make on our pockets, and happily vote for them again.

I appear to be at the receiving end of a blame culture, those 'it's all Yahoo's fault, Madam,' assurances beginning to wear thin by now but it got me off their backs each time I accessed them until I could garner sufficient strength to have another go. I could learn a thing or two from BT, other than the practice of patience and control.

Truth be known I was running out of patience but steadfastly holding on to control, when constantly thanked for my patience, to which I had to politely respond with 'Thank-you!' or some such trivial acknowledgement or the phrase was repeated until I did respond.

I idly wondered, when trying to shut out the eternal music, quietly exercising control, would the people whom I now thought of as colleagues on the other end of the line, become as familiar to me as the man Himself, after he decided 10 long years ago, he would become my boss. All we had to do to elicit a response from each other when meeting up during our working routine was for him to say, 'Uh Huh!' and me to reply, 'Mm Hmm!' That was much more honestly satisfying than BT's thank-you for your patience nonsense. At times of real stress Himself would sigh, 'Man, man!' and I would answer, 'Yes. Indeed!' and on we would go, in total sympathy with each other's plight without the requirement of knowing anything about each other's problem. A highly stress free working practice I could franchise to BT, and a few others I could mention.

To keep me on the line these dear distant colleagues also changed my browser and anything else that came up their speculative hump, repeatedly, time and time again, trying to force my email to access its account by accepting a password it had already adamantly said it was having nothing to do with. Two hours down the line, on yet another occasion, I once more had a solid promise I would get a call back. To date not one materialised so I was a little sceptical, but as I had to exercise control, I kept my opinions to myself.

By now I had an empty house, no paying guests, which was as well, as the next day saw me back at throwing up at the very thought of India, a country I had hitherto enjoyed travelling in. Himself, in an act of magnanimous kindness suggested that seeing we now had no guests to care for, he would take me out for a meal. Oh, that would be nice, I thought. Get away from it all. What a nice man.

'Where do you fancy going?' Oh, wow! Free choice. Mmmmmm. My spirits were rising by the second. 'Either The Captain's Galley, or Forss House,' I grinned back, salivating at the thought of an evening in either of our award-winning local restaurants, my mind racing. I mustn't look too enthused though, just put-upon enough to be the one who did not have to do the driving home, ready to be cheered by a good bottle of expensive wine.

'Oh,' the dear man replied, his inviting smile fading. 'Do you not fancy an Indian, then?' This met with such a wave of condemnation, we thought it more prudent I stay at home to practice better control of myself. I think I mentioned his deviousness before.

The cats were still skulking from various corners of the garden, appreciating the fact it had turned into more of a wild-life jungle than ever as I absented myself from all but the essential of manning the telephone, to honour my side of the agreement that when India phoned back, I would be here to take the call. They were very adamant I adhere to that particular rule. 'You will be there Madam, when I call back.' It was not a question.

Nothing daunted, next day I was determined I would speak with someone and held on for an inordinately long, long wait. I got the precious human answer, my voice cracking on a sob as I listened to the person I thought just might have the familiarity of a British accent, regardless of nationality. But it came again from that distant continent, which was a bit of a surprise as this time I had tried Customer Care again, determined to wait, however long it took, not realising it too was farmed to a foreign call centre. She cared enough to tell me to control myself…Madam. It must be a phrase from their rule book I concluded. In pretty fast order, Customer Care cared only to transfer me to the Indian call centre internet department. Thereafter followed a long call, about another hour added to the initial wait, followed by a wild gallop through the full explanatory performance again. I then had to hand over the pc to my new Advisor and watch yet another abortive attempt to force the account to accept a password it had repeatedly said it did not know and was not about to be persuaded to change its mind. After a few less than in control comments from me, about this being Yahoo's fault, I was transferred to the lower ranks of Yahoo and assured by Yahoo all would be well because this would now go to the highest levels at Yahoo. This delay in sorting the problem, he agreed, was not good enough. Tsk, tsk, you could visualise the chap saying. They would fix it and call me back. I felt I was getting somewhere at last. 'Yahoo!' I shouted in triumph as I leapt off my chair. The cat retaliated by leaping at the window in a desperate bid to get out.

Actually, one good aspect of the whole sorry saga – the cats were much less inclined to spend time fighting in my office over which one was going to sit on the hp photosmart, or assist the passage of the paper into the printer, or turn off my wireless connection, as had happened in the past, when I was new to the technicalities and contacted India to say I couldn't get online. After the obligatory long session to ascertain who I was and what could possibly be wrong, the puzzled question came, 'Do you have wireless switched on Madam?' and red-faced, full of apologies, I would tap the wireless connection key. It took time to suss out the culprit as she daintily trotted over the laptop trying to avoid being shouted at when standing on the alphabet keys. Pooh insisted it was therefore not her fault she stood on the wireless connection key and I should allow her walk where she wanted and then she would not disconnect me.

When Yahoo eventually rang, merely to remind me they were looking at the problem, I managed to control myself sufficiently to say in an even tone, 'You can't tell me why this has happened. You can't tell me how long it will take to fix. You can't even tell me what the problem is, other than BT saying it's Yahoo's fault. When I ask to speak with whoever is responsible at Yahoo you tell me that even you are not allowed to speak with the higher ranks at Yahoo, yet you are Yahoo!'

At least I was now connected to the people – not the top people because that was not allowed, only the lower ranks – who were actually admitting it was their fault, so some progress had been made. And do you know what this important Yahoo fellow did? He changed my password and spent half an hour trying to force it down the internet's throat. Then he changed the browser, and said, 'Do not worry Madam, we are fixing the problem.'

Keeping a tight grip on control, I replied quietly, 'No, you are not.'

'This time it will be fixed, Madam, because it is going to the highest levels at Yahoo.'

And this time I got a cross-my-heart-and-hope-to-die promise that between 7.15pm and 7.45pm on the following evening, thus giving the highest echelons at Yahoo their necessary 24 hours to fix the problem, I would get a call back telling me that all would be well. And do you know what? I believed him. I filled in the Happy Form saying although the problem remained unresolved, the advisor had been ever so good.

That night saw no bums in beds once again with the lump under the mattresses diminishing before my pain-filled eyes. Times were getting hard. I took on a worrying attitude: rejoicing in the peace to answer the phone to explain to those who bothered to enquire, why I had not answered their emails. Instead of being angered that British Telecom was sabotaging my business and despairing at the empty coffers to match the empty rooms, I felt relieved I did not have guests to worry about too.

I waited for the Yahoo call. I even changed my attire into some-thing smart and efficient, and brushed my teeth, Yahoo being of such high rank. The call never came. But two hours later, would you believe, a call from India. A very clear voiced individual with a 'this must be all your own fault' attitude, informed me he was Yahoo and yes, it was a Yahoo problem but it would be fixed this time because it was being 'escalated' to the highest levels at Yahoo. That information, of course, took at least 20 minutes to impart and of course, I had the temerity to mention that the problem had already been up there with the Yahoo gods, to no avail.

I would get a call back between 7.00pm and 8.00pm the following evening.

'Do you mind if I don't dress up this time?' I quietly asked.

'Pardon?'

'Oh, never mind,' I sighed.

I didn't bother dressing up. I was back in teenage years, convinced I was dealing with a poorly chosen boyfriend who was showing his true colours once he had me hooked. I waited, and true to expectations, no call came, so I sat and documented the procedure and drafted a politically correct, politely stroppy letter to Sir Christopher Bland, the Chairman of British Telecom.

Just as I completed this, after 10.00pm, India called, two hours outside the specified time. 'Do not worry, Madam. We are fixing the problem. We will call you back tomorrow.' They just called to say they were on the case. Wasn't that sweet of them. I sweetly told them I was on the case too and Sir Christopher would sort out BT and Yahoo together. After all, he holidayed in this beautiful area of Scotland so he must appreciate the depressed effect such inefficiency could have on our economy. This met with a stunned silence and the most quizzical 'Pardon?' to date.

I said it was okay, I was no longer that fussed. My attention span was slipping after all this time. He said, very quietly, at 1.45pm I would be called back. 'Are you BT or Yahoo?' I asked. Back to BT it appeared. So I told him that one of his colleagues had given me a telephone number, which I was assured, would not involve long waiting, to ask if BT would set up another email address so I could get information out, as I could not get into my account. I had tried this and was put on the inevitable hold after keying in the requisite numbers supposed to serve my specific needs, which I construed as 'sales' but I could have been wrong.

'That is an incorrect number,' I was told in a relieved voice, because this he could deal with though in a manner contrived to imply it was I who was at fault, not they for giving out wrong numbers. 'That is why you had to wait a long time. I will give you a number you will not have to wait on,' and he gave a different number, said I must ring now and would get an answer. 'It's 11 o'clock at night here, and you've exhausted me. Tonight I want to sleep. I can't face any more waits and problems, not tonight,' I wailed, fearful of being told to control myself, but such advice had come from the female handbook as the male of the species had never mentioned control.

It was an 0845 number of course, but the heart had gone out of me and I began to believe I could live well enough without communicating with anyone and really was not very sure if I ever wanted an email address again. Did I even want paying guests? I would have no business to speak of as July was a prime time to fill up the autumn spaces through email enquiries. Did I really want a dribble of business, courtesy of BT, when I was used to a busy household, through copious funds going into advertising using this email address, I debated? Stuff it! I no longer cared. I was feeling quite gung-ho, went to bed and slept soundly for the first time in a week.

Next day, enough was enough and I decided it was time to phone a friend. She used to work with BT and was a whiz-kid at fixing any problem with an internet connection. A super person, patience and kindness meted out in equal measure every time I brought her my computer disasters when I first went online many years ago at a time when my pc took the most hellish exception to being asked to do something it obviously thought was not in its remit, and terminally crashed, taking all my work with it. Moira saw this as par for the course, took it all in her stride, found all my work, had it transferred to discs and soon onto my first laptop! Magic! Himself referred to her as my Magic Friend!

It was little wonder visitors loved staying in her welcoming B&B! She also had a fantastic cat that got everyone into trouble before they discovered it was she who swung on the door handles, opening them willy-nilly, appearing in places she had no right to be, no doubt quietly grinning to herself as cats do when they cause a kerfuffle. I only just learned, days after writing this, when still trying to get my account with BT sorted, whilst speaking to Moira and asking after Jenny the Cat, the sad news Jenny was involved in a road accident and had to have her leg amputated. Moira says she is now well recovered and back to her usual tricks!

When I first started writing my monthly tourism column for the Scottish Provincial Press, and set it out with a mix of hard information interspersed with interesting happenings and an anecdotal finale, it was she, at a networking lunch, who gave me my very first 'funny' and appears here as written in the *Northern Times* weekly edition:

> And Finally...
>
> A colleague who was 'fair chuffed' with the benefits derived from providing accommodation over the lean winter months for the decommissioning trade at Dounreay, attended a course run by Caithness & Sutherland Enterprise.
>
> The tutor asked what exact level of business they would require, to ensure an acceptable profit.
>
> My friend quickly answered, 'Oh, I'd be well satisfied with six men every night.' There was a stunned silence until the tutor managed to reply, 'I bet you would!'

I gave her my tale of woe and within 10 minutes she rang back. 'Yahoo have locked you out of your Account. You need to speak with them as BT cannot sort that, despite them working together under Btyahoo.com.' It was the first explanation I had been given other than eventually to be told it was not the fault of BT but the fault of Yahoo, though no one actually said Yahoo locked me out of my account. She could not understand why, it being a simple single email account, mine the only name on it.

She then went on to tell me that she had just survived a nightmare situation with British Telecom herself, but she at least had the contact details to go ballistic at the right person. They had sold her account to another user! Just like that! She was furious and nobody told her to control herself. Fortunately she was able to contact a friend in the system who could safeguard her account from that instant, neverthe-less it was a horrendous experience. For days a British operator who sorted out everything to her satisfaction called to ensure there was no continuing problem following such a disastrous action.

Her friend could do nothing for me because the fault lay with Yahoo. I told her I was actually in contact with Yahoo who had little to say except repeat BT's mantra, 'Do not worry, Madam, we are fixing the problem.' Never mind, on the next specified day, only five minutes late, a call came from another rather officious chap. I asked him if he was BT or Yahoo, after he told me the problem was still ongoing – as if I required telling, but they had to say something when they rang up, I suppose. He said with great dignity, 'I am Btyahoo, and do not worry Madam, we are fixing the problem. We will call you back in 48 hours.'

And that is where I sit, on my hands most of the time, waiting for more catastrophic happenings and if you are not thoroughly bored by the whole sorry tale, then I am, so that is where I will leave it and get on to something, anything with a more uplifting flick to its tail.

Oh, the Manns, on the doorstep. Just another by-product that must be dealt with by spending forever finding good accommodation for disgruntled people who think they are booked here. The Manns had never made the booking, which was something of a relief when we sat rifling through their paperwork. At less busy times I look at the great empty spaces in my register and sigh, saying to myself, 'Do not worry, Madam, someone is sorting it out somewhere.' I think longingly of the middle of October when I will be gloriously free of all such concerns. After 40 years, I thought the home-straight of the last few months in this business would be a time I would thoroughly enjoy. Courtesy of British Telecom, it has become a nightmare.

I wonder if I shall continue to be locked out of my account, with daily build-ups of emails coming in from all over the world, until the end of my career. There appears, or so they tell me, to be no way of contacting these enquirers to tell them of the situation when I set up a new email address, with a new service provider, of course. Maybe I'll miss my friendly Indian colleagues more than I'll miss all the guests! By then I shall probably be incarcerated for failing to control myself properly when writing to Sir Christopher. I wonder too, how much is in his pay packet for standing rap for that lot, poor man.

It is now more than 14 days into the fault and all I get are brief updates, very polite, faithfully asking after my health in the first instance, then explaining that the fault – except they do not refer to it as a fault: it is a problem – is ongoing. And then they close the conversation by saying, in their lovely quiet sing-song voices, 'Do not worry, Madam. The problem will be resolved and we will contact you in another 24 to 48 hours. Thank you for using BT broadband as your server.'

8

Bitten By The Standardisation Bug!

I'M CONVINCED I HAVE it sussed now. In fact, the enigmatic smile I've had to cultivate in order to back up my new-found sense of control may well rival the Mona Lisa. I'm trying not to bite the head off the innocent guest, who for the hundredth time this year, on learning of the impending retirement, says with a touch of sadness, 'You won't know what to do with yourself, will you!'

My answers have run the gauntlet of the ambitious plans laid aside to be accomplished sometime in the future; the new house to be built; our home to be sold; at least one book to be supported through active marketing (or so I assured the publisher); more books to write; friends and family to catch up on – if they remember who I am, that is – and so the exciting list runs on. All this is in the recesses of a mind that adamantly refuses to rise to the bait of, 'Oh, you're going to miss this terribly, aren't you?'

I, through politeness have to answer, 'Of course I am. I'll miss the people that's for sure,' and refrain from adding, 'only some of them'. No way will I miss the work, the devoted and dedicated attention to detail that is one of the attractions of the establishment along with the hospitality. Funny thing is, I *will* miss dishing out hospitality and cooking breakfasts, the more complicated and diverse, the better I like it.

And therein lies a tale that had much of the B&B fraternity at war, if not with each other, then with VisitScotland. When proprietors belong to their Quality Assurance Scheme, the criteria pertaining to each graded level – in VisitScotland's case stars were the symbols used to denote standards – have to be met. This allows advertising through VisitScotland lists, including the visitscotland.com website as well as many opportunities to put adverts in a variety of brochures covering all of Scotland, which go out to the domestic and oversees markets.

Everyone has agreed for years that symbols (the diamonds, crowns, stars or whatever) each scheme choose to identify the quality of an establishment's services, should be standardised into a single identifiable recognisable icon such as VisitScotland's stars. It took an inordinate amount of work for all the agencies involved to come together: the Welsh Tourist Board with their dragons; the English Tourist Board with their attitude; VisitScotland with all its security of knowledge that many countries now, like South Africa, are adopting their star scheme; the AA and RAC with their resentment; so that all would, by 2006, go forward under a new standardised rating. This in itself raised all sorts of difficulties, with many believing that Scotland dropped its very high standards to meet with the AA, who were known to dish out diamonds in a less stringent manner. It was believed, too, that other areas of Britain sometimes fell behind Scotland in its quality standards in accommodation.

Not that you would have thought so when, as a member of the VisitScotland Overseeing Committee, I sat and listened to the first presentation made by a consultative company from across the border, who unblushingly told us how standardisation was being introduced so we could all catch up with the excellent work of the English Tourist Board. We were left open-mouthed, our English-born colleagues taking more exception to this pronouncement than us natives. Probably because they were more aware of the vast difference in standards and how difficult it was going to be, to introduce the star ratings – at that time it was not even agreed that it would be stars – without dropping standards in Scotland. On the other hand, he may just have been winding us all up and making a good job of it.

Success would be difficult, but achievable, and in its bringing about, inspectors who had years ago metamorphosed into advisors, and the Executive who ran the Quality Standards Scheme at VisitScotland, used the opportunity to introduce what they saw as even better standards in some aspects of the delivery of 'the tourism product'.

As ever, this led the bed and breakfast sector to feel they were hit by a mind-set that had little understanding of the way it delivered some of its finest traditions. The discipline involved was the service of breakfast in the four and five star establishments; the one - three Star rated B&Bs were allowed to retain their status quo. There was sufficient ambiguity in the newly laid down guidelines to ensure advice was sought by those who wanted to see a clearer ruling so the operator knew which method the new criteria supported.

The difference of opinion arose because one or two operators and some quality advisors believed that breakfast orders should not be taken the night before in higher rated B&Bs. The opinions of the visitors did not appear to come into this as no one could come up with a complaint, and those who made a great job of the pre-ordered breakfasts knew well that their guests were very happy with the arrangement.

The most puzzling aspect of these deliberations was that it hit the operators who delivered the finest of choices coupled with an ability to cook diverse and difficult breakfasts. Thus the new ruling to do away with previous night ordering appeared to support those who were producing a standard breakfast within a reasonable time-scale in the morning, or a more complicated menu which required a long wait. This leaves a question mark over just how fresh ingredients may be if the previous day's diners had not ordered these dishes and they lay yet another day in the fridge. If the fridge was stocked on spec, offering a variety of choices each day, what were the chances all fresh food would be consumed every morning? And would that which was not ordered be ditched and more fresh choices bought in, on the off-chance it would be eaten every day? That being the case, those who say they diligently cook to order and give a wide choice have either money to burn or a very cheesed off family, who must suffer every day from a diet of left-overs.

Since many a long year it has been traditional, and therefore fully expected, for bed and breakfast operators to show their guests the breakfast menu in the evening and ask if they would identify their choice of main course. The exception is the, much to be avoided, host who produces no menu at all but asks, 'Do you want the cooked breakfast?' in a tone of voice portraying how happy she or he would be if you were to decline. It was Hobson's choice and even today, there are travellers who tell us, because they refused the 'cooked' breakfast, they sat down to a miserly slice of white toast and a few cornflakes along with a single glass of orange coloured liquid! The so-called 'cooked' breakfast invariably being nothing more exciting than sausage, bacon and egg!

And then of course, there are the tick lists, reminding us of a stay in hospital. Even down to whether or not you want butter, each item ticked off is presented to the guest next day exactly as ticked, with a frown if they felt you overdid the ticking! Preserve us from being ticked off with such a practice, and from the undercooked sausages and bacon, done in a rush after the order is given in the morning, or worse, the micro-waved sausages and bacon, or micro defrosted then flash cooked. Then again, some cook their sausages then freeze them before a quick defrost and flash in the oven. The possibilities are end-less, and each less palatable than the one before.

We all have our different ways and opinions but if the end result is an obviously well-cooked and delicious breakfast, with no com-plaints coming from guests, then why change it? Complaints arise more often due to poorly cooked breakfasts, poor choice and poor attitude. That is what the QA people have been concentrating on improving, but in doing so they are changing a well tried and trusted method of pleasing the visitor.

If I take you through our own set-up, a set-up I have won accolades and awards for, you may understand my questioning of this particular change, without consultation with the people it affected most, the visitors! It's a small thing by comparison to the vast consultation that has been done with the visitor by VisitScotland as their much vaunted research is testimony to, but remember, we are talking about Bed and Breakfast, and if the Bed is no good, and the Breakfast is no good either, then what have we other than a roof over your head, ready next day to endorse that adage: a bad experience is reiterated 10 times more than a good one!

We have always presented the menu the evening before with great discussions on the sourcing of local food, various methods of cooking and what exactly are some of the ingredients that make up a dish; it is an integral part of the stay enjoyed very much by the guests. The menu we have used for some years now is backed up by coloured pictures of the main courses and fruit dishes, so everyone knows just what they are ordering. It is explained that despite the menu lay out, there is no either/or section, so that guests can have as much as they want and mix items from one dish to another as they please. A few days ago a young man who sighed he was not 'into' breakfasts said, when I lifted a plate, 'I can't believe that is my third course and I still have to get my salmon!' He only had a bowl of fresh fruit, followed by home-made yoghurt with compote, then porridge and cream, before the scrambled eggs and smoked salmon, to me, a normal order. 'Yes, and after that,' I seriously told him, 'You're not allowed to leave the table until you sample some of the home baking!'

Breakfast is fun; the ordering, the cooking, the serving and the eating of it. There would be no fun whatsoever in providing a much depleted menu, with absolutely no time for a leisurely discussion of ingredients, sources, and who makes what locally. I would be so busy cooking to order, whilst taking the inevitable telephone calls that interrupt constantly, and serving all to the table. It would be too rushed for any of the banter that lightens the mornings. Take today for example.

'That was a fantastic sleep,' avowed a guest.

'Yes, I put kelpie dust under your pillows,' I quipped back, then told them, when they laughed, obviously knowing I was teasing, 'I'm going to have to stop telling my guests lies. The other day we had someone back with us and, inevitably, when someone said they had a great sleep, I mentioned the kelpie dust and our repeat visitor said, 'That reminds me. I tried everywhere to get that kelpie dust and no one seems to have heard of it. Where do you get it?"

For those of you not in the know, the kelpie is one of our Highland water nymphs, a bit irascible. It's better to keep on his good side. I never thought to be taken seriously!

Imagine taking six orders from the following menu and the American style refrigeration you would require to furnish requests if all, for instance, decided upon the haddock and poached eggs of a morning. And what would you do with all the other ingredients not used:

Breakfast Menu

Pure Orange and Pure Grapefruit Juices
Variety of Cereals including Superior Muesli and Bran
Prunes with Apple, Rhubarb & Raspberries, Grapefruit Segments
Raspberries, Blackcurrants, Strawberries, Blueberries when in season
Freshly cut mixture of Soft Fruits

* * *

Local Golspie Milled Oatmeal Porridge
Homemade Natural Yoghurt with Fruit Preserve

* * *

The Sheiling Fry Up – with locally sourced ingredients
(Bacon, Sausage, Fried Bread, Tomato, Mushroom, Black Pudding, Haggis)
Goujons of Fresh Herring rolled in Oatmeal & served with Sour Gooseberry Sauce
Lightly cooked Natural Oak Smoked Haddock with Poached Eggs
Scrambled Eggs with Melba Toast & Smoked Salmon or with Grilled Bacon
Natural Smoked Loch Fyne Kipper cooked in its own Juices

Cheese & Onion Omelette
French Toast with Spiced Tomatoes
Poached Eggs with Toast or Grilled Bacon & Tomato
Two Boiled Eggs

* * *

Home Made White Bread & Brown Wholemeal with
Scotch Pancakes and Scones
Scottish Oatcakes
Highland Wildflower Honey
Homemade Marmalade
Home-Made Preserves from Local Fruits

* * *

Fresh Brewed Ground Roast Coffee
Ground Decaffeinated Coffee
Hot Chocolate
Pot of Loose Scottish Tea served with Hot Water
Earl Grey – Decaffeinated – Fruit Teas – Fresh Lemon Slices

Always, the guest is asked if they are happy to give their order the previous evening and it is made clear that a change of heart in the morning is perfectly acceptable; this should never be seen as a problem. Only the main and the overnight soaked porridge require ordering.

It was extremely rare to have any say they would prefer to order in the morning, the offer made so as to comply with this VisitScotland request that orders be taken only in the morning. I continued to argue I would not devalue the breakfast I had won awards for, and was one of my best marketing tools, but I met them half way and compiled a different menu for those who wanted to order in the morning. There was a reasonable choice on this menu, but nothing like the main menu perused the night before. In the couple of years the short menu was issued alongside the other, two couples used it, and next night they joined in the food discussions and ordered from the original!

We never used the microwave at breakfast, ever, but often took the wonderful, fat, succulent Loch Fyne kippers out of the freezer for ourselves and cooked them in the micro for lunch. They were good but not nearly so delicious as the long slow cooking process I used in the mornings. That kept them juicy and with no kippery smell permeating through the house. The kipper had to be the only fish dish I would cook to a morning order as it seemed to cope with the shock of micro defrosting. Eggs in any form, and bacon, mushroom and tomato could be rustled up, cooked in the traditional frying and grilling way if guests were happy to wait. We did not use the oven to cook bacon or sausages. My only moan was the time it took to peel the tomatoes ordered at the breakfast table, previous night orders peeled in the earlier part of the morning along with other preparations. The times I gave in to temptation and left the tomato skins on, a little pile of skin would be returned with an accusing look.

One particular couple, who did not want to order the night before, arrived early and as they studied eating out options for evening meals and our own breakfast menus over their afternoon tea I couldn't help thinking the man rather aggressive and argumentative, a University lecturer, retired, he proudly informed! He was good craic though and I enjoyed his spirited opinions on life. His wife was one of those very sweet people who constantly smile at you and are very agreeable. I thought, poor woman, dominated by her opinionated spouse. He's giving her a right hard time and her so patient and quiet! I soon discovered there was nothing poor about her and any hard time given was by the lady herself, always accompanied by a quiet, martyr-like smile!

Before retiring for the night my other two parties had happily discussed all the food and made interesting choices. I serve the table as well as cook the breakfasts, Himself deciding at the start of his new career, there were certain tricks old dogs like him could not cope with. Serving table has been something that has never brought a change of heart, despite his desire to do a silver service of afternoon tea, right up until 10.00pm which was a bit of a mind-set change for me to get used to. My problem was, I had yet to set eyes on this Rule Book for Old Dogs he assiduously stuck to.

Next morning I dealt with the teas and coffees – we use loose leaf tea which has to be handled differently to tea bags but is much appreciated as a lovely change for most people, except ourselves, the quick tea bag sufficing!

'Oh, dear! Can we get a fresh pot of tea. The bag seems to have burst in the pot!' Some of them had never witnessed a tea leaf in their entire lives.

My chirpy retired teacher, excuse me, lecturer, gave his order for tea and his sweetly smiling wife looked at me with pity expressing the desire for Earl Grey, which she doubted we would have, despite it being in the bedroom hospitality tray selection, and offered on the menu.

'A pot of hot water will do me' she added before I could assure her she would have her Earl Grey. It was on the menu, but she seemed to have an aversion to looking at menus! It could be a cultural nicety I was ignorant of as she studiously ignored its appearance at the table. Mr Peel suddenly decided there was so much fruit to chose from, cereals etc and home-made breads, scones and pancakes, oatcakes too, he would skip the main course altogether. Good man, I thought which was not my usual attitude to any decision not to eat heartily. I devised the popular French Toast and Spiced Tomatoes to meet the challenge of young ladies who would not take a main course. This, they happily consumed as did many others over the years, with the bright-eyed comment, 'Oh, it reminds me of home when I was little!' or 'It's like being back at boarding school.'

Mrs Peel decided she would have a yoghurt, provided the accompanying compote was strawberry. She hit it on the head. It could just as easily have been blackcurrant, or rhubarb and apple, as no way was I preparing a choice of compotes every morning.

'And to follow?' I enquired, expectantly, menu in hand, ready to reel off the considerable items I could do quickly in the morning. I was itching to get back to the cooker to ensure guests who had ordered the night before would not have their food spoiled because of her dithering and insistence I wait while she thought about looking at the menu.

'I'm not quite sure yet. I'll know after I have some fruit,' came her eventual response, accompanied by a wide smile that never quite reached her eyes. I could have cried, and somehow I think she knew that.

The word control-freak flashed across my mind but I dismissed it. Not gentle Mrs Peel. One had ways of playing up the control freak type, but I couldn't bring myself to play up this ever-smiling, genteel lady.

By the time they left, I was quite ready to do just that! Eventually, about half an hour into the breakfast she decided upon scrambled eggs and a little grilled bacon! Her smiling requests were met with determined charm, though I soon reassessed her smile as more of a leer, my own response moving towards a bearing of teeth, whilst Himself did a dance of annoyance in the kitchen at the sight of all the pans he had just cleaned and put away reappearing, gas ignited and grill on full – a dangerous situation.

There's a fair distance from kitchen to dining-room with quiet music in the area between, conning you into believing nothing can be heard emanating from the kitchen. Not but that there's plenty to say there, especially after Himself decided to change a few of the routines I had found so helpful in my job before I acquired a boss. Just the other day, I touched a hot plate, got burnt, and very quietly commented, 'Oh my, goodness, that *is* hot,' well, words to that effect, and when I served the offending plate, a guest asked, 'Did you burn yourself, my dear?' I could hardly answer for wondering what other little gems floated in there over the years!

The boss' spirited response to the kitchen still having all the accoutrements of cooking lying about instead of packed away had to be kept to a whisper. This was totally unsatisfactory to the situation, so he shot out the back door and roared at the outside walls, frightening the cats who believed the garden sacrosanct from such irrational behaviour, never before having heard it from the male of the species. Their next venture into the kitchen saw them circling him rather cautiously, something I did myself quite often.

The close confines of a B&B should demand training that ensures all angst is kept away from the delicate ears of guests. A proprietor who was not exactly known for her good nature housed a very large number of guests and could be as cantankerous to them as she was to her staff. One morning, with a full to overflowing house, things were particularly fraught. A young hiking couple asked for sandwiches, which were offered in the advertising to be sure, but madam flew out of the kitchen and told them in no uncertain terms what she thought, believing they should have given the order the night before. They could do without. A single gentleman particularly irritated her too with his fastidious behaviour and likes and dislikes. As it transpired, after a noisy and fearful end to the breakfast service, it turned out he was an Inspector from the Tourist Board but his triumph was short lived as he pounced with his card. It can't be too often they catch anyone out so blatantly doing what so many knew was going on in some establishments. As he valiantly attempted to imbue a better attitude, he ended up being flung out on his ear, never to darken her door again, and she got off with it! I couldn't help but admire her spirit when I heard the story from a chortling member of staff. That same Inspector told me about it himself, years later, and I laughed even more then. He admitted, in retrospect, he'd had many a laugh over it, but at the time it appalled him!

'Having the nerve to throw you out, never to darken her door again, or being so mean to the guests?' I managed to ask, grinning.

'I think both,' he told me, sighing at the memory. They do have fun, those Inspectors! Those were the days long before their adventures came to light in reality TV shows. Shows many people involved in the industry cannot bear to watch, the standards of hospitality and facilities so obnoxious it is too painful to endure. I actually met one of those hotel inspectors from the TV who had just bought a copy of *Heads on Pillows*. I was too embarrassed to admit I never watched these programmes, which he was certain would be grist to my mill.

Getting back to Mrs Peel, I knew I had no option but to put up with her irascibility, and would never have got off with telling her to sling her hook. I was determined not to be forced into treating her different from everyone else. Nevertheless, I was grateful that morning to my other four guests who ordered some really interesting dishes because, before Mr Peel left the table, he announced to all and sundry, 'Tomorrow, I shall have that,' pointing to Goujons of Herring in Oatmeal with Gooseberry Sauce!

'My goodness! That's the earliest order I have ever taken,' I crowed while the smiling one retained her dignity along with her stance and played up every morning, and at other times too, always with that same sweet smile. Her husband and I had some wide-ranging discussions. By the time they were ready to leave and he came to say his goodbyes, I was sorry to see him go. For her, the goodbye was said earlier, frost sparkling from the ever-present smile.

Mr Peel completely shocked me by saying this was by far one of the two best places they ever stayed at, the other being on the West Coast. *That* establishment, he impressed, took their breakfast orders in the morning but the food was not near so good as here, and true, when the company was not interesting, waiting could be a bit of a bind. However, it was a real good place and I would now join it in meeting his high standards.

'We shall definitely be back,' he assured me.

'You're very welcome,' I sincerely told him, and with the biggest smile I could muster, sighed happily and added, 'but you'd better bring a different woman if you want to stay here again,' and I meant it. He actually laughed all the way out the door, but he never, to my knowledge, attempted to come back. I suspect he dined out on that one to the chagrin of his smiling better half!

Arguing the case for evening pre-orders of breakfasts I found myself at loggerheads with one of the top officers at VisitScotland who avowed he would hate to give an order the previous evening.

'No porridge for you then, at my place, and no choice of fish either!'

'That wouldn't bother me,' he said good-naturedly, 'but no porridge! That's ridiculous! It doesn't take that long to cook. You make the point about wasting food, but surely you could afford the few pence each portion of porridge would cost had it to be thrown away unused.'

'When did you last buy quality oatmeal? And when did you last make proper porridge?' was all I could say to that, our debate continuing to the meeting table. He made some fair points, as did I, so before we left, I capitulated sufficiently to devise the alternative menu. He agreed this would be very acceptable. It lies, however, in the menu folder, overlooked and underused. And I'm glad. With only three months to go now, visitors have yet to say they have breakfasted better elsewhere. To achieve this takes a very early rising, with a lot of time given to prepare all the fresh ingredients, and a great deal of dedicated shopping. For us, it is well worth the hassle and it seems our guests think so too.

By the same token though, I am certain other proprietors must think we waste a huge amount of fresh fruits because of the huge choice we put on each morning, and always freshly cut that day. Our sacrifice is that what the guests leave, we have for breakfast next day instead of having the usual fresh cut we have at other times of the year. And of course the garden rhubarb keeps for several days, cooked to perfection without a strand mushed, as if taken out of a tin. This is achieved by using the lowest possible defrosting heat on the microwave and cooking for more than an hour.

So, when it ain't broke, why mend it is all I can say to anyone who wants to change some traditional aspects that continue to serve the visitor to their satisfaction. Or do some people really think that when we take the orders the night before, we actually cook the breakfast then, to save time in the morning? Think of the lovely lie-ins we could have would be Connie's answer to that.

9

The Haunted Room

ALL THE BEST HOUSES have one. It didn't dawn on me for a long time that we too had one, or at least sported some kind of spirit locked quietly in the confines of a particular room. Until out of the blue, as is the way with these things, it made its presence felt through its own particular style of manifestation. For years I thought it the vagaries of the job until it dawned on me that such calamities were prone to happen only in *that* room.

Nothing was ever seen, nor did I boast its existence. That would not have been good for trade, contrary to the turreted and castellated accommodations that draw in the crowds because of their resident ghost. A ghost has to put in appearances, usually about the beginning of each season, just like the Loch Ness Monster, so as to retain its place in the market, to entice you to book in and be the one to see it. Most ghosts are obliging, as is the Loch Ness Monster, but mine was not at all of the obliging sort.

I doubt it is a poltergeist – no one wants ownership of one of those whilst offering peace and tranquillity in a Highland glen. I suspect it's more a left-over remnant of a stay by a long–gone-to-the-other-side person I used as a guinea pig when learning this job. Now they are getting their own back with a sense of, *see-how-she'll-cope-with-this-then* humour. Until now, I have kept this unpredictable presence hushed.

By the time you read this, I shall be retired and, as you know, the best of people come out from under the woodpile in a tell-all frenzy and highly lucrative publication, once they retire from a situation. Be it a relationship or a parliamentary performance, it is then you get the gist of things that have gone bump, whether in the night or during the day. Sadly, my tell-all tales are more interesting than possessive of sensational appeal, so even though I'm telling you, I know there's no money in it. 'I'll just tell you for the craic,' a friend is wont to say before delivering a juicy bit of information, always with the caveat, 'Now, remember, you never heard that from me, because I don't gossip!'

My invisible antagonist confines its activities to one room and can be neither felt by cold rushes of air nor by any ectoplasmic manifestations not the work of an artistic spider exhibiting skills in a particularly difficult and distant corner. Waiting for Himself to demand I wield the feather duster in case an Inspector calls.

Things just happen in that room making me wonder, why? Nothing ever occurs in any other room to render me prostrate with apologies, involving me in a situation I would much rather enlivened someone else's day while I laugh my socks off. Take for instance the case of the American and the trousers.

Americans can be delightful people and we have had a great many stay with us over the years. But they do have some idiosyncrasies, pertinent to that particular nationality that would give away their country of origin even if you knew nothing else about them. The only question then is, are they from the good old US of A or possibly Canada? Canadians have tendencies towards the same habits but in a milder form. One aspect of this inclination is to arrive for breakfast, settle down, and then for the duration of the meal, float back and fore between bedroom and table for no obvious reason. Smiling vaguely whilst getting under everyone's feet, especially mine when they suddenly appear, congeniality oozing, into the kitchen.

Not all do this, but many are very mobile during breakfast whereas few other nationalities indulge in such a consistent exercise programme. I am convinced that is all it is, a way of ensuring they are not inflicted with a thrombosis during the meal. It's very considerate really, as such an interruption to the breakfast routine could not possibly enhance an establishment's reputation: klaxons blaring from rushing ambulances and police sirens attracting attention a good address would prefer not to boast.

The room that keeps catching me out is the first we ever had on offer and housed one of our earliest parties of friends travelling together. That trio of identical little women who sat on my couch, each a mirror image of the other, feet neither touching the floor nor backs requiring support, for all the world like three brown speckled bantams roosting on a *spàrdan*. You may have read in *Heads on Pillows*, they so bewitched my husband he threw in the towel and, after several months of shying away from such a terrifying commitment as B&B (making statements like, 'Over my dead body,') in my absence offered them our one bedroom. Producing them to my astonished gaze when I returned from a walk to the shop, with a conjurer's flourish.

I could have happily produced the requisite dead body, for these three rabbits could not be popped back into the hat and I was stuck with them instead of accompanying him to a happily anticipated night out, by me anyway. As for him, nights out were approached with a sideways search for a good excuse not to go. And he had found one! The deviousness of the man! Especially a man who worked away from home and studiously ignored the fact I had started out on this rather dubious method of earning some pin money after leaving my *proper* job to produce our first, and only, child. I was supposed to have the weekends off. We were never supposed to have these frightening people in the house when he was home. Now he had broken the bargain so from then on in, he had no option but to fully capitulate! My devious man was part of the venture whether he liked it or not!

That room then, all of 40 years ago, had three single beds and little else other than matching bedcovers, curtains, two chairs – the third person could sit on the floor, there being no Scottish Tourist Board in existence to demand a chair for each bum – a dressing table and two bedside cabinets, a fitted carpet, and a poor specimen at that. This lack of amenities was not a miserly offering. People had little, and little was expected, other than cleanliness and a genuine welcome. The going rate for bedspaces being all of 5/- per person – 25p in today's money. In truth, from day one I was lucky in being able to offer a great deal more than in most places, the house being new and furnished with the growing needs of young couples who wanted more than their parents.

Today the room boasts an en suite shower room, a king-size double bed with top of the range linen, good furniture as well as a top quality wool carpet and window drapes with matching bedspread. The cost of the bedspread alone would have easily furnished my lounge back then, leave alone a bedroom. There is also the hospitality tray stacked with all the goodies now expected in most B&Bs. Along with such facilities it also houses my high spirited ghost.

The morning of the American fiasco, I had served a full table of guests their breakfast but a small spillage required a clean napkin so I headed for the kitchen. The drawer was empty. Never mind, I had a stash in the linen-cupboard. At that time this cupboard was situated beside a wardrobe, one of a built-in pair in the bedroom I mention; the cupboard space not required by guests as the wardrobe was adequate to their requirements. They also had another store cupboard, now empty of the fold-away bed once incarcerated there, and though I told the story in *Heads on Pillows* of the 'Manuel' look-alike from Fawlty Towers who gave me a night to remember involving that room, I never let on I suspected a less worldly presence to have instigated the farce.

In a rush to get back to the table, I hurried into the American's room and quickly opened the linen-cupboard door. That all lighting was left full on and the en suite fan running was par for the course when you entered a room vacated by Americans, so I thought little of it. Reaching out for the napkins, I heard a distinct rustle. I cocked my head to a side thinking surely not. A mouse? It sounded remarkably like the rustling scamper heard at times coming from the loft in the dead of night. Himself would have to be commandeered to take charge of the mouse-traps while I remonstrated with Felix, the cat.

Very quietly interrupting my castigating verdict on the cat's working habits, I heard the unexpected strains of Yankee Doodle Dandy softly whistled. My heart stopped. I sneaked a tentative look over my shoulder and there, with the en suite door wide open, a pair of long skinny legs emerged from trousers pooled on the floor, the rest of the person obscured by a newspaper that did not even twitch as the occupant sat it out.

Slowly closing the cupboard door, averting my face and with eyes focused dead ahead, I sallied forth from the room, humming at a level that drowned out Yankee Doodle, the rousing strains of *Scotland The Brave*.

I hadn't seen it. I wasn't in the room. I would banish the picture from my mind forever. That was the only way I could face the table again when I produced the napkin, too late noting the empty place. Later, waltzing in to collect the breakfast plates from all, including my American gentleman who was back at table, as happy as a sand-boy, I had to concentrate hard to subdue the image that kept threatening to explode in raucous laughter.

It was that room too that saw The Hobbit (the only tomcat to compliment our household, and susceptible to bouts of madness) play out one of his favourite games when the hunting was poor and indoor pursuits proved more entertaining – and you'll note I am at pains not to lay claim to owning a cat, these independent creatures choose to live with us, as and when they like. That day I had newly served afternoon tea to a lovely elderly couple, very typical of the refined British guest who tends to holiday with us in the quieter months of the year. Their expectation is always high and their appreciation graciously made known. They are, without exception, a pleasure to care for.

The Hobbit tried to sneak into the forbidden territory of the lounge when I put my head round the door to ascertain all was well with the MacAndrews. The cat then raced upstairs to hide, but with all doors up there closed I left him and opened the glass fire door in the hallway to do something in that area. I always leave doors open to the bedrooms waiting for the new arrivals but just as the fire door slowly closed, Hobby nicked through – he had this movement down to a fine art as do all three cats – and shot into the vacant bedroom. I tore in after him. The cats were never allowed into guest areas for many reasons, and certainly not guest bedrooms, not unless specifically invited by the occupant, a habit thoroughly discouraged by me. Give a cat an inch and it has a mile tucked under its paw while you wait.

There was only one place he could be. Under the bed and sure enough, crouched in there, huge green eyes leering out from a handsomely striped face, he defied every pleading request to come out. Cats respond well to bargaining but I appeared to have nothing he wanted this time.

In the act of getting back on my feet, I gave vent to my feelings with an explosive, 'Oh, Balls!' just as I spotted a pair of male feet in the doorway, beside which were the female pair, beautifully and expensively shod. Rising slowly and thinking fast, I looked at this cultured couple and said, 'Balls! I've just remembered. I forgot to make the butter balls for the breakfast table. I must run and do it. It's one of these jobs we can get out of the way early,' I gabbled, fingers crossed behind my back, as Mr MacAndrew ushered his dignified wife into the other bedroom. He then turned round and broadly smiled at me whilst the cat sauntered out of the room, tail waving on high and if not quite a grin on his cheeky face, then a definite look of one-upmanship. It had all happened in *that* room.

We had two bedrooms to let by the time we owned one of the first house-rabbits known, long before they became a fashion item with pet shops selling all sorts of play areas and resting places to amuse the rabbit while enjoying the confines of the house. Which was, I suppose, much better than enjoying the confines of a hutch. Our rabbit, Bendy, was confined to nowhere. He arrived unexpectedly, all of 37 years ago, and had the freedom of not only the house but the hills, coming and going as he saw fit.

He grew from a tiny ball of black fluff into a huge buck rabbit, Rex breed with massively long ears, extremely attractive as well as dominant by nature. He sorted out guest dogs with alacrity and told my own bold terrier just where to go. He was, though, very well behaved, never destroying anything in the house, clean as a sixpence, always asking out to the toilet and was well loved by everyone, especially the children of the village. When he met his untimely death, I was gifted a rabbit specially bred for me by Neil, my policeman cousin. He owned and showed Silver Foxes but mated his breeding doe with a colleague's Black Rex and the result was a gorgeous black, fluffier and smaller version of our beloved Bendy. This bunny never interfered with guest dogs but spent a great deal of time with the housecat Puss-Do who arrived long before Felix and the trio we have today. Both house-cat and rabbit were unusually friendly with a foursome of young feral cats, who roamed the grounds, our pets spending many a night out of doors with this wild feline pride.

Rex was also the most mischievous creature I ever knew, then or since. He took great notions to certain guests and followed an Australian girl about like a puppy. In the middle of the night her screams could have been heard a mile off and rushing to her rescue I encountered in the corridor our north of England guest who shared *that* room with his wife and young daughter. It transpired that when we believed Rex out for the night with the cats, he had hidden under the Australian girl's bed and pounced upon her in the middle of the night, thus causing terror not only to the girl but to the rest of us! He was banished with a severe warning, something he was well used to, cocking a snoop at us as he skipped out the door.

One of his little pastimes to draw attention was to sit quietly in the hallway where guests paid their bills. What he was actually doing was gnawing on the corner of the wall until he got a tiny piece of wall-paper well gripped, then he would rip, the noise alerting every-one, but he would be off – we had no fire-door then partitioning the hallway from the bedroom corridor – paper firmly held between large buck teeth, heading for any door left open.

As he ripped wallpaper, my heart would sink. My job, after getting the appropriated booty off him, was to painstakingly glue the tattered piece back on the wall before Himself came home. He and Rex were not the best of mates. The rabbit teased the man of the house beyond endurance at times and more often than not I found myself acting as defence council, battling with a beady-eyed judge, black cap in hand, to have him prepared for next day's dinner or banished to the colonies. He had already been incarcerated in a hutch my father made for him when I pled sanctuary for my errant wee pal after a few bouts of high drama delinquency. Naturally, I appealed and got him out of jail, back to lopping into the house as often as not while the feral cats took to sleeping in his hutch. Mornings often saw those wild creatures fly out of the hutch, followed by a sedately bored looking Puss-Do, then Rex, who must have slept at the bottom of the heap, hopping out, as if this were normal leporine behaviour. It is good I had witnesses to such wild-life exhibitions or no one would believe it. They were great friends except when Rex accompanied their hunting forays and Puss-Do would persistently try to turn him back, to no avail. We would watch from a window as the ferals walked the old broken-down, moss-covered stone dykes, followed by Puss-Do, every few yards turning back, trying to be rid of the rabbit thumping along at the rear; ruining any hope of silently capturing the rodent residents of the old tumbled down dykes.

On one occasion it was the Yorkshire family who were paying their bill and it was to their bedroom, the one that causes all the consternation, the rabbit fled to as the mother and daughter were about to vacate the room. In a flash, he was under a bed with the wallpaper firmly gripped between his teeth. The game was usually up when I entered into the spirit of things and crawled to wherever he had taken his loot, which could be anything portable he snatched. He would then let me have the stolen goods, until the next time.

I raced after Rex into the bedroom and found it very difficult to even see where he was under the confines of the bed, but I spotted the long strip of pale paper, still in his teeth, in the dark gloom that melted into the black fur of his coat.

'I'll get him in a minute,' I assured.

'I'll get t' little booger now for you,' my North Yorkshire guest insisted, brandishing a broom he had taken from the kitchen.

I was horrified. 'Don't you take that brush to my rabbit,' I gasped, trying to take a dignified stance which proved rather difficult as his wife hopped around and his little girl watched goggle-eyed from the other bed.

'He's been nowt but trouble since we came. I never heard the likes. They're bloody vermin where I come from!' growled the irate man, getting down on his knees, broom in hand until I wrestled it from him.

Rex flashed past us, paper still in mouth, haring up the corridor, me hard on his heels firmly clutching the broom, my guest convinced he could overtake me and get at the rabbit.

'We're not used to rabbits in the house,' his wife whined, taking up the rear whilst the little girl informed us all, 'When I go home, I'm going to get a black rabbit just like Rex.' I have a feeling she never did.

That too was the room where I lost the bright red toe-nail, the whole incident detailed in *Heads on Pillows,* leaving me with an anxiety complex that should really have had psychiatric treatment but there was never time. Stabled horses are wonderful listeners when things go wrong and as they were partially to blame for the loss of the nail, I took my troubles to them. Bronco advised, find someone to blame and then convince yourself it's all their fault. So I put it down to the mischievous spirit and it's amazing how the anxiety goes and the incident is tucked in the recesses of the mind, when you lay the blame elsewhere.

It wasn't long before our first grandchild was dogging my foot-steps as I tore through the rooms and prepared the house for its daily changes. Looking back, it is always that one particular room that threw spanners into our hectic schedule. His mother often gave a hand, allowing me to attend meetings by doing rooms and bookings for me. On one of her first mornings, Skimbleshanks hadn't a look in as Shane watched us with considered doubt written all over his face.

'*Not* to touch the radio!' he pointed out as she tackled *that* room. Quite right too, as I used to explain procedures to him, just to keep him interested and stop the perpetual questioning, like, 'Why did gestis do that mess?' He became the recipient of all sorts of interesting snippets, for a small child, as I managed to keep my reaction level as congenial as necessary, refraining from throwing a fit in the middle of the floor. I knew full well he had the ability to tackle a guest for anything that drew such interesting behaviour from his granny – yells of, 'Oh, sugar! What next will I find!' or words to that effect had to be curtailed. Next thing, when I was all sweetness and light, he would throw into the conversation, 'Gwanny was wild today. Hers was in your room sorting the mess.'

However, he remembered one rule very well and told Katrina, in no uncertain terms, '*Not* to fart in the bedrooms!'

'Why not?' she asked, a twinkle in those beautiful sea-green eyes. Being an earth-mother of exemplar ability, nothing a child said would throw her.

'Cause the gestis come back and go, sniff, sniff, and think it's Gwanny what did it!'

I believe I did warn him off such behaviour when he went through this phase of running to find me to make sure I was suitably impressed with his ability in that direction.

His other best remembered incident left me vacuuming that room after telling him to go and play as I was really, really, busy. I happened to look out of the window and saw what I was sure would be visitors, heading for their car. I switched off, ready to call them back and met my little helper in the corridor. 'It's okay, Gwanny. I told Gestis you was too busy ho'oring in the bedroom!'

There were many memorable incidents involving that room but this last was only a few days ago and from now on I shall never look at a certain flower again with the nostalgia I once held. Now I see the marguerite from a completely different angle. Passing the problem bedroom door, quite late the other evening, it opened and Anita, one of our German guests, popped her head out. 'I must tell you,' she said, her face a picture of deep concern, 'that in this room, you have everything I expect to find in a good German hotel. I travel a lot.'

Oh good, I thought, as I had imagined by her body language there was something wrong. I was premature in my relief.

'You come in,' she implored, opening the door wide, 'I explain something you do not have.' It sounded serious. She was clad for bed in wonderfully bright red plaid pyjamas, this warm material a typical choice for so many of our guests who come from European countries, especially Germany and Sweden. They wear the most unglamorous night attire, copious, with thick warm fabric despite our bed linen being ultra comfortable next to the skin and our rooms as warm as they would wish. But then, maybe all places are not the same, as we do get told how cold it can be in certain hard-nosed establishments where there's a propensity to turn off heating by date, regardless of weather conditions and artfully contrive to keep it off until some late date in October. That's why you see hot-water-bottles in rooms in the scorching hot weather we do get more often than is announced by our errant weather forecasters. 'Be prepared' had to be the motto of my lovely German guest as she beckoned me to step inside.

By now I could feel my anxiety levels rising when I noticed her other half just about ready to get into bed, but being a gentlemen, he invited me to come in and patted the bed. Oh, god, this is going to be seriously bad when I have to sit down was all I could think.

'You have so much to give us,' Anita continued, 'and I must tell you that Roland has taken me to many places in your country and this has been my favourite.' I was swinging from relief to worry in equal measure.

'But now I have to tell you about this one thing,' and she made her way into the en suite. My heart stopped. If anything were to go wrong, it would have to be in that vicinity. Sod's law again. This is where things happen, things that may not be fixed in seconds, having to wait to call out a plumber or electrician in the morning. The evil law that governs so much of my life ensures things happen at night, or next best thing, a Saturday afternoon, or Sunday. We were lucky, having a large attractive main bathroom within a few yards, feet in this case, of the bedrooms, which was used only on rare occasions, and could be a back-up if anything went wrong with an en suite during a stay. But everything in working order was a much better situation, though I have to say that our electrician, Dougie, is a treasure, worth his weight in gold, coming out at all times to ensure all is well. We've been lucky with our plumbers too, but even then, in the countryside, you can expect a wait.

'So,' Anita continued now she had both Roland and I all crowded into the en suite with her. 'In Germany, when you go to use the toilet...' she stopped to look seriously at me.

It was going to be bad! I prepared myself for the worst. She was probably going to say, it usually flushes and this one does not! How awful! They had newly arrived early that day and were probably patiently waiting for the cistern to fill up, thinking, everything takes time in Scotland.

With measured emphasis, she continued, 'You lift the lid,' she demonstrated, 'and in Germany, you smile!'

That you should be so lucky! Not some of the lids I've been know to lift, more like cry than smile, I thought, still on tenterhooks. I knew no such shock had awaited them as they lifted this lid, doing the cleaning myself every day. The old dog as ever was relying on his book of tricks that said such activity was prohibited, to be carried out only under extreme duress, preferably by the underdog.

But her next statement totally threw me. 'What do you do when you see a beautiful big flower...you call it the marguerite? White, with lovely yellow centre? Yes?'

My eyes widened as I looked up at Roland. He was smiling.

'You smile!' she enthused to my blank response, spreading her arms wide and looking into the toilet pan, big grin on her face.

Well yes, I do actually smile, but the memory that makes me smile is of the smaller marguerite, the one we grew up to know as the dog daisy. The field next to our home in Kirtomy was white with them by late summer. My sister, Sandra, being three and a bit – that bit always an important power-base when you are a child – years older than me, had precedence over decisions. Therefore when we were supposed to be curled up in our beds at night, it was she who was out romping among the marguerites and I who was nominated to stay behind because someone had to help the escapee back up the wall and in through our bedroom window.

She was eventually caught when she spread her wings further afield and a dereliction of duty saw me fall asleep before she was ready to abandon her play. No way could she get back in of her own accord, our bedroom being on an upper floor, with conveniently placed window above a stone wall aiding such escapades until our deception came to a spanking end. But I often remember her long, thick, wavy, golden hair and pale nightie glowing in the moon-light as she played while the white flower heads of the dog daisies bobbed in the gentle breezes we seemed to have in those long gone summer nights. It was a fond memory, now forever sullied.

'In Germany,' Anita at last informed me, 'when you lift the lid of the toilet, there, floating in the water is the head of a marguerite! Only in good hotels. And you smile! It is good. Yes?'

'Yes,' I agreed, smiling too, more in relief, but I was thinking, wait until I wind up some of my colleagues and tell them that there is a new criterion for the higher rated accommodations to retain their four and five star status: VisitScotland now insists that toilet bowls have a marguerite flower head floating in the water to greet new guests!

If it causes a fraction of the indignation and downright determination not to comply with all that some of VisitScotland's ideas have brought about, ideas that are now an accepted addition to add value to a stay, it would be worth the ruse, just to hear, 'Well! That's it this time! That's me finished with them. Never mind the welcome at the door, the tea offered, the warmth and what have you. Just so long as you have a bloody flower stuffed down the toilet pan to greet the guests!'

In my front garden, in full bloom at this moment, are two clumps of flowers remarkably like marguerites, the legacy of Pat Rodlin, a horticulturist who lived in Skerray, a fascinating and beautiful crofting village on the north coast seaboard, working as hard as any to develop an area of our coastline using many traditional methods. It is she who cultivated this strain of flower, growing profusely in our climate, reminding us of that hard-working woman, who succumbed to the ravages of cancer, leaving many to mourn her loss.

That flower head fits the bill perfectly, but until I travel in Germany and see for myself this floral contribution to all that makes a stay memorable, it is not a practice I shall take up. Just in case the German sense of humour was encouraged by my spirited ghost, it being some time since it caught me out in *that* room.

10

The Sound Of Silence

SILENCE MAY NOT BE the objective of all who enjoy peace and quiet. Just think of diners sitting in hushed surroundings, frightened to discuss intimate matters with companions for fear each word is heard by the ever so quiet customers at tables clustered together for convenience of staff, in some corner of a vast old-fashioned dining-room. A similar situation can arise in B&Bs, especially in places where the traditional convivial table has evolved into separate tables for each party of guests, grouped through necessity, rather close to each other. A shared table encourages chat, especially when the host ensures the ambience is good whether on a quiet level or the hilarity that makes serving a happy table one of the better parts of the job.

A bit of decent, quiet background music is a clever camouflage, provided it is not one of British Telecom's preferred recordings that blast your ears for weeks on end, interrupted by the Eastern promise, 'Do not worry, Madam, we are fixing the problem.' I am now well into my third week of listening to the same set piece; I know it by heart and like it less each time I hear it – and ditto to the set-piece assurances; not one whit closer to getting back my email address which it appears from recent conversations had been given to someone else who deleted it. BT had me believing, during another long five day discussion with India, I would actually be getting back my original marketing email address, the one they at last admitted was deleted.

By whom was not so easily confessed, though they had to agree it was not I who was the guilty party. I had no proof they had sold the address on to another. I wondered why 'another' had got it, then deleted it, but such questioning involved far too many 'Pardons?' so I gave up and rejoiced in the fact, I could get it back.

I was ecstatic, ready to forgive all in the excitement of achieving an end to the problem. Arrangements were made, time consuming arrangements, to set up the new account the following day. I went to bed with a smile on my face that was still there in the morning, replacing the lump of anxiety I now wakened to, wondering what BT had in store for me each day. Later that day, told to me merely as an aside, along with the oft repeated assurances, I found myself right back at square one when I heard the following statement filter down the line; 'Madam, do not worry, we are fixing the problem and today you will get your email address back. I will set it up now.'

'The Sheiling at btinternet dot com,' I happily concurred, the words rolling off my tongue in eternal gratitude.

'Em, no Madam, it will not be *exactly* the same address...' That's as far as he got before I bit his head off. He did not tell me to control myself but went dead silent until I changed tack and said, 'Thank you for your patience and for holding the line,' and waited until he responded properly and politely before I continued. 'I have put more than £1,500 out on advertising that specific email address in hard copy literature which is circulating its way around the globe and from which I am supposed to earn a living. I have put 40 years of reputation into being marketed in several prestigious publications you cannot buy your way into, veritable bibles for the travelling public, and they give out that specific email address. If I cannot get my exact email address back, you can stuff it.' On reflection, I am glad I did not add '...where the monkey put his nuts!' when I listen to the furore in cricketing circles after one player called the other 'a Monkey!' and got accused of base racial prejudice.

'Pardon?' he said, and I went silent. I considered putting down the phone but he broke into my dark contemplation and asked, 'Do you want me to set up the email address now, Madam?'

'Yes, if it is exactly the same address, for the obvious reason, that I have used in my advertising. Please do it now, this minute, instantly, immediately and without delay, thank you.' I wished it had been a woman so I could have added, Madam. Sir, does not quite have the same ring to it.

'Madam, I cannot set up the exact address. I am telling you always Madam, it cannot be the same address. It takes up to 100 days to get that exact address back.'

Rather pointless at this stage but I did check it out and apparently it is true. To get an email address back after an account is deleted, notwithstanding the time it takes – for me, well over two weeks – to find out why this had actually happened, plus the couple of days trying to persuade me I had deleted the account myself. As if! Going into my account – which I never do anyway because there's never been a need to change addresses or passwords and I never have the time to muck about with the computer – and cutting my financial throat, ruining my reputation as a business woman and a reliable board member, chairman etc etc. Then came the welcome BT admittance, that, no, I had not done the dirty deed myself, but BT were only *partially* to blame. Remember, Yahoo was the big boy who did it, then ran away! The audacity of him!

Another peculiarity, purely to outwit, this 100 days lark allows BT to sort out the technical aspect of the problem, but I discovered to my chagrin, 100 days is the time limit Ofcom allows British Telecom to deal with a complaint before you are considered ill-served enough to have your desperate situation heeded! And like the '*call you back within 48 hours*' scenario, you are encouraged to think the account will be set up well within this stipulated time. For me, the 48 hours proved fictitious, so I have little hope for the 100 days to perform better. At least now I felt justified in settling down to the legalities of the situation with a few well-worded letters, other than my correspondence to the Chairman of British Telecom for which I had yet to receive an acknowledgement. If it did not jeopardise my case, with my warped sense of humour, I might be tempted to say, what fun!

As to silence-blasting music being the preferred treatment to which customers are subjected while on hold, why doesn't BT have a wee prayer session or something productive, more encouraging, for their clients to listen to while they hold the line? And if that is alien to the nature of the caller, a workshop on new words to adopt when frustrated. Lots of alternatives spring to mind.

All calls to BT broadband may be recorded for training purposes. If you wish to hear a prayer, key one; if you wish to extend your knowledge of the vernacular, key two; if you wish to listen to the Encyclopaedia Britannica whilst on hold, key three; if you wish to catch up on a sleep session, key four for lullabies. If you require advice on how to control yourself, key five. You are speaking today to the Tooth Fairy! Thank you for using BT broadband as your preferred service provider.'

But I must tell you this, read in the Daily Express newspaper at the weekend, and I quote:

Business woman (name given) told yesterday how she was kept waiting on a BT helpline for 20 hours. Mrs K rang the phone company after a line she had paid for was not installed at her new flat in (address given).

She rang them three times, twice waiting eight hours, and then gave up after a last, four-hour stint of listening to piped music and recorded messages.

Mrs K, who has now been prescribed sedatives, said: 'I was so frustrated I broke down in tears.'

She never mentioned being told to control herself. If you remember, I actually was reduced to tears, after a mammoth hold and at last heard a real person speak. Fat lot of good that did me. BT Customer Care at its best.

But I did get one laugh out of it. Frustrated beyond belief by the dreadful music, I pounced on the Advisor when next put on hold, 'Don't! Just don't put me on hold listening to that diabolical music yet again.'

So he didn't, but instead I heard a cacophony of voices as he and his colleagues jabbered away whilst 'fixing the problem', or so they assured me. At one stage, they asked me to ensure the blue broadband wireless light was still on. 'Oh, no,' I said, totally dismayed. It was off and I hadn't noticed. 'It's that damned cat again. She's gone and switched it off. I can't believe I didn't notice that.' Pooh must have walked over and hit her favourite key again without me noticing and I felt such a fool. Because there was no music to hide their voices, I distinctly heard some words spoken, then, 'It was the cat!' followed by howls of laughter, then several loud 'Meows!' filtered down the line. The meows went on for some time. I'm convinced they forgot that I was not sitting listening to music but to them and I could not help laughing to myself as it sounded terribly funny. They seemed highly tickled with the cat's behaviour. Resetting the key did not fix the problem, but at least I went off the line feeling I was dealing with youngsters who found ways of enlivening their working day, just as we did ourselves when young and carefree. It certainly lightened that particular episode but taught me it was better to put up with the music than hear their comments, just in case they reverted to English and gave me as good a character as I gave them at times.

To get back to providing good music for your guests, a service very much appreciated and carried out willy-nilly for years, until Big Brother caught up with us all. Out of the blue, which is a change from out of Europe, came the directive that no public area should produce copyright music without a licence issued by the Performing Rights Society. Operators of small B&Bs believed themselves outwith this ruling because of the private nature of their homes. That cuts no ice with the licensing authorities. I thought myself well out of it by using my own music and songs, copyright fully paid up when recordings were made, but sole infliction of my voice could have lost me good business so I confessed to being as guilty as everyone else in supplying an eclectic mix of entertainment each and every morning.

But, music must not be played to paying guests without procuring a licence, full stop! Has threats of damages and costs, and the Designs and Patent Act 1988 for copyright infringement driven this very large sector of the tourism industry scurrying to buy rather expensive licences? Oh, I'm sure it has; I would hate to cast aspersions on my colleagues. Me personally, no, because, my own music being dicey, the music I play is for the express purpose of soothing my nerves as I cope with the problems of the day – and Poodie-Pooh, our girl cat, is rather into hearing classical music of a morning. I cannot help it if a paying guest listens. Conscientiously, I suggest the use of ear plugs, so as to keep on the correct side of the law, but I cannot enforce their use. I wonder if the Performing Rights Society has the same clout as those who enforce the smoking ban, then I could call in the authorities and force my guests to wear ear plugs, or come to the table while using their own personal stereos. Would make a change from the growing tendency to have the mobile phone as the preferred break-fast companion.

Should a guest waltz about your premises with fag in hand, belching out smoke, and you are incensed enough to call the police, you're barking at the wrong enforcer. It is the province of the Local Authorities, and that's a laugh, to sort out the offender. You would be better off with the Railway Police who appear to be the only ones who come to grips with the criminal as he or she defies the law.

As for BT, I would advocate they have their licence revoked for cruelty to innocent members of the public, who must listen to what they construe as suitable music. However, what they construe as suitable service, is in my opinion, and that of every single person with whom I've spoken, open to serious doubt.

We all have different ideas as to what constitutes an annoying noise and what is music to the ears. Take the dawn chorus, for instance, enjoyed by the vast majority, but not so one of my guests, a lady from France who was asked if she slept well.

'I sleep very well, until the birds start crying so early in the morning. Their very loud cries wake me up!' Maybe another cock-robin had fallen foul of a wayward sparrow, with his bow and arrow and she had tuned into the wake!

Apart from the food and hospitality, our main marketing tool has been a guarantee of absolute peace and quiet, knowing it astounds people. All is so still and silent from the moment the household settles, usually between 10.00pm and 11.00pm, at times well before that, until the guests themselves come to life in the morning. Himself and myself are very skilled at flitting about quietly from around 5.30am, and a sound-proof glass fire-door ensures no kitchen chaos carries to the dining-room or guest bedrooms, our own bedroom and shower-room are outwith that area altogether. It's a lovely time in the morning with the golden sunrises we get, along with that special light in the north, drawing so many delighted comments from visitors. We often wish our guests had the pleasure of enjoying this too. But on the other hand we are happy they are tucked into their beds, well away from the inevitable interruptions as we get on with preparing all the fresh fruits, breads and other ingredients to make up what a guest referred to recently, in the visitor's book, as 'a banquet fit for a king'! Other things may go awry but the food is, without exception, of the best.

The exceptions that caused embarrassment came in breaking that golden silence, remembering we've been foolish enough to guarantee it! The nerve to advertise silence came through the knowledge our guests were of the quieter type, no business people or workmen staying to disturb with their different starts in the morning, and beer-fuelled noisy toilet flushing in the night. There are only the two of us living in the house, often just myself, before I got a boss. Cats, despite many other ways of making their presence felt, are silent creatures. Especially Smudge and The Hobbit, while Pooh thoroughly enjoys long conversations and will have the last word however much you are prepared to test her vocal stamina. But they are kept out of guest areas, which is easy during the silent sleeping hours. Except, of course, when Pooh has been listening to some operatic music and goes out to perform at a nearby cat's concert emulating the singers. Now that can be quite disturbing.

'Was that one of your cats, screeching out there till all hours last night?'

'Oh, no. That would be the screech owl or some other nocturnal bird, or it may have been a fox. We get lots of night birds. And foxes. Definitely not the cat.' Mental note to kill cat later, looking at the red-eyed gent from the room nearest the cat's concert area. Yet, hearing he could have been the recipient of a wild-life nocturnal exhibition spread a huge smile across his face, in place of the tight-lipped enquiry when he thought it was my cat who had disturbed his sleep. Attitude again, told you everything in the tourism industry is based on attitude.

Such disruptions are very rare, so little disturbs the guarantee of peace and quiet but, with *that* room having to give its resident spirit a bit of free reign every now and again, something has to go bump in the night. What happened last season proved the biggest bump that ever happened in the history of this house!

I am a particularly light sleeper, indeed since adopting a different lifestyle involving a great deal of worry after contracting cancer, I lost the ability to sleep through the night undisturbed as I used to, with few exceptions.

We had a couple stay for two nights and in the morning when Mrs White arrived first in the dining-room, I nipped in to ask if she had slept well. I was smiling. She was not.

'Yes,' she answered, but without the expected conviction, then added with a wry grin, 'We got back to sleep and slept very well after it all quietened down.' My smile faded.

'After it quietened down?' visions of some wild partying filtering through open window but from where? Did Pooh have one of her concerts? I'm usually up like a shot after the first ululation, threatening dire retribution in the morning if they don't pack it in instantly. It seems to work during the summer months with all such performances reserved for wild cacophonic nights during the early spring. I put up with these, in gratitude for the noise-free environment I boast during the season.

Mrs White looked at me in wonder. 'The noise. Didn't you hear it? Have you not seen your bathroom?' The incredulous tone should have warned me.

'No,' I honestly answered, there being no need for me to go into that area of the house, 'But I never heard any noise. The bathroom? What's wrong with the bathroom?'

'You better come and see,' was all she said, turning her back and leading the way.

The door to our large main bathroom is often left ajar which had allowed her to discover the source of the midnight disaster. I could not believe my eyes. Knowing I had abandoned pans for a quick word with Mrs White, I gulped, closed the door, shook my head at her and took off for the kitchen, stunned into silence. No doubt my eyes were bulging in shock.

Meeting the other four guests, as they came in, I tentatively asked if they slept well. Like babies, they all agreed. A colicky baby or a sweet dreams baby, I was left to wonder, but further questions proved they too had heard nothing. How we had slept through it, I shall never know.

I never mentioned a thing to Himself as he studiously got on with his side of the breakfast-preparation bargain. He would just have flown into Skimbleshanks mode and had us all in there picking plaster and debris off the floor with breakfast allowed only after we had cleared up the mess to his satisfaction. This would have taken at least up to breakfast time the next day by the look of things.

It was a nightmare. A white plaster decorated ceiling had fallen in, with tons of water-soaked insulation and chunks of plasterboard strewn around reminiscent of a Turner Prize entry. Could we be harbouring Tracey Emin, in disguise, practising her toilet theme? Whatever! It was complete ruination of what had been an eye-catching and much admired room. One area, through an archway remained intact, as if flaunting its pristine condition at the chaos on the other side. The only blessing was that this bathroom was not required by guests, so bookings were not affected. My insurance company was very glad to hear that. But where had the water damage come from, never even noticed because of the style of the ceiling?

Skimbleshanks to the rescue. After his shock, when breakfast was safely served and I escorted him to the scene, beckoning rather than explaining, his deafness being a degree worse if you dragged him from his work for no good reason. I had attempted to explain but was left feeling like Chicken Licken when she had to tell all the other Farmyard Animals that the sky was falling in. Himself didn't really believe me and put my hysterical gesticulations down to too much sun the day before. I wasn't used to getting out into the sun.

With great patience he painstakingly tested every water source, me acting plumber's mate. Not that I felt very matey, but I jumped to the commands coming fast and furious; flushing toilets, taps and showers for hours, until our upstairs shower proved the culprit. Though looking intact, the seal in a tiny area actually allowed some water to filter through, building its load over a long period of time to dump with a vengeance at midnight. The only porcelain to be damaged was the bath, tiny dimples in the quality material all good suites came in over 40 years ago. They were barely noticeable, and though the insurers said they would replace it, the thought of hauling out the bath proved prohibitive and we went ahead with the repairs and redecoration instead. Fortunately, for the sake of the delicate part of the anatomy that makes contact with the dimpled interior, there are no sharp edges!

That was not my only worry. I, personally and with no real excuse, broke my own golden rule that ensured peace and quiet with no small children allowed to run riot, no harassed parents, and no fractious crying in the night when prepared to pay for a five star quiet stay. So, sorry, no little children allowed. It's too risky, although I found the decision hard, loving the wee souls, and never having a single one do anything wrong in all the days we enjoyed housing families when we offered more rooms. I always enjoyed the entertainment value most children give when encouraged by interest in what they have to say. But this time I had been persuaded to accept the booking of a young couple who didn't bother to mention she was pregnant. Why should they. None of my business, except by the time they booked in, baby had well and truly arrived! They were so excited to have their tiny tot in a carry cot to show off rather than hidden away in his lovely mother's tummy, I agreed to honour the two night reservation. How could you say no! That did not stop me from being extremely anxious. They arrived the day the ceiling caved in. However, the Whites who had suffered the dumping of the ceiling the night before, upon being given the news we had a tiny baby on the premises, seemed philosophical about it and the parents had assured, she was a very quiet little girl. The bedrooms are fairly soundproof, but I still worried.

Next morning, having heard not a cheep from the baby, confidence brimming, I asked the mandatory question to a rather sour-faced Mrs White.

'I'm afraid we did not,' came the surly reply.

'I never heard the baby,' I frowned.

'No. You wouldn't have because the baby never made a sound. It's the parents who spoiled our night's sleep and if I hear that tune played again, I'll scream!'

Partying? Jeepers! Again, how did I not hear it. Pooh's wild mimicry was tuneless (don't ever tell her I said that), so it couldn't have been her.

'They had music playing half the night!'

I could have wept, but instead thought, I'll kill them. It must have been unduly loud to have filtered through closed doors and down a corridor! I went back to the kitchen absolutely deflated, hardly able to believe that a house which could boast silence for near 40 years just had to have two catastrophes on the two nights a couple had come for peace and quiet.

By the time I spotted the young father nip out to his car, I felt so annoyed, I never gave a thought to asking him first if he were the culprit. I just pounced.

'Why were you playing music so loud in the night?' I demanded to know.

He raised his brows and said, 'It wasn't us. It came from another room. Must have been your other guests?'

'No. It was they who complained and there are only the four of you and the baby staying.'

'Well, it wasn't us, but I did hear it.'

I was profuse with my apologies, both for the accusation and the disturbance. 'It didn't bother us, and it went off after a while,' he assured, as realisation dawned on me. The door to the empty room was open, the blessed alarm had been left on, defaulting to midnight because the electricity was off when we were scouting for the water leakage. It had been on for an hour from midnight. Extremely irritating, although in the end the Whites were okay about it and had a lovely time at the table with the family after I explained it was all my fault and reparation would be made!

It wasn't my fault, but like all good proprietors, I accept blame. It was that damned apparition at it again. The music had come from *that* room. It is now August and it must know it has less than three months to go if it wants to keep up its well-earned reputation. I just wonder what it can manage as a finale to top that!

Which reminds me. BT called again today. Wasn't that nice!

11

And Another First

WITH READING HIGH on my relaxation agenda, and biographical books a firm favourite, a story written by a couple who grew daffodils was finished, not with the usual satisfaction of laying down a well-written book with a contented sigh, I instead felt totally anxious on the writer's behalf. The book was crafted in a manner ensuring you suffered their disasters along with them, page, after page, after page, sticking with it to the bitter end. It was only bitter because I was convinced I would rejoice with them when at last it would all pan out. As things got worse and every new venture was met with soul destroying failure – tiny gains wiped out by the next kick in the teeth – I built up expectations, believing when at last they got the venture up and running successfully, I would feel a measure of their triumph and rejoice with them as I turned the last page.

That didn't happen. Now I fear that with each new development with BT I am putting my reader through similar exasperation, chucking this book aside with a despairing, 'We're never going to get an end to this, are we!' Bear with me through my trials and tribulations because there is light at the end of the tunnel, though I'll be back in another tunnel if I continue down the road to litigation. The stress is bound to get worse, the very thought making me want to run in the opposite direction, but being an eternal optimist, I believe justice will be mine if I take the legal advice given and accept I have a good case.

What I was given today was reason to understand why the kidnapped fall in love with their kidnappers! Being a hostage to the miseries of the last three weeks at the hands of my BT captors, the prospect of being set free has left me euphorically thankful to a dear man from the Indian call centre. It definitely was not he who was meowing at me the week before, I know that. His lovely eastern voice and assurances of all being well, when at last I saw every re-connection light flashing, made me feel like throwing my arms in the air and shouting down the line, 'BT, I love you!' Now that would have been a first... for BT, I'm sure!

But to another very important first, when this card arrived in the post, an official looking card, informing me if I wanted a certain piece of mail, I should hasten to the Post Office with £1.24 clutched in my anxious little paw, and pay them for the service of handing the mystery package over to me. An unusual happening at the best of times, the last time being letters from the land owner of the croft we tenant, and instead of paying the due sum for the Unpaid Deficient Postage, to give it its proper title, we found out the contents from the few who had received a legitimately stamped letter, and told the Post Office they could keep the mail. Or open it up and return it to sender and get them to pay the travel expenses of the letter.

For me it was a day I had been greatly looking forward to. My favourite family, Dr Bill and Mrs Joan Gunnyeon and their two sons, along with their relevant partners, were due to arrive, so the ominous looking card was set aside until the next day. Joan and Bill first came into our lives all of 19 years ago, with their two young boys, Malcolm and Kenneth, when they 'chanced' booking a holiday through seeing our advert in one of the Tourist Board publications. We've seen them most years ever since. In good years more than once, although eventually without the boys when they went upon their own much more interesting ways in life.

Talk was often had of how it would be great to have them all back, and now it was actually happening, all six taking over the house for a long weekend. A first, no other family has ever managed to fill all the rooms, allowing for that much loved house-party atmosphere of many years back when dinner was served up every evening, guests coming back early to dress up and congregate in one of the lounges well before dinner time. Drinks in hands, bonhomie flowing, and appetites honed by recapturing the events of the day, reminding me of safaris when each of us would vie to outdo the other in what wonders our day had delivered.

On one or two rare occasions since giving up serving dinners, which I had cooked for 28 years, I wanted to treat certain guests, but this was difficult because there were always others staying. When I tried this, the private meal was served in the dining area of our own sitting room, some distance from kitchen and guest lounge, office and all activity, which meant I had to scoot back and forth, attending others and answering doorbell and phone calls, turning me into a whirling dervish of activity rather than the serene hostess I should have been.

Although everyone else had a great time, I seldom did, but of course could not say so. This is a breeze, had to be written all over my face, though almost washed off by the sweat coursing down my brow!

However, this time, the Gunnyeons would be taking over all rooms and I determined to host an on-the-house dinner, despite Bill's protestations he would pay, as he had always done in the past. One thing was for certain though, we were all delighted we were re-establishing an old tradition and I won the day by saying, if Bill paid, Himself and myself would not be joining them, any more than we had in the past! So, the meal was planned for the eight of us, for the Saturday night, the day after their arrival.

As for BT, that fickle lot appeared to have forgotten my existence when I made the decision to take the huff and no longer call them, after demanding a written explanation as to why my account was deleted. I also wrote to cancel my direct debit, explaining I would pay by cheque when the bill came, but it had better not include a charge for the time I was not receiving their service and I would not expect to pay for the many and lengthy fruitless 0845 calls. I had set up a new address, courtesy of my friend Moira, on my website, contacted those I felt it imperative knew the new address and stopped hanging about the house like an anxious lover, waiting for the 'full of Eastern Promise' call-backs.

The new email address did nothing for my business, a high percentage of enquiries coming from VisitScotland publications, and many others, out in hard copy where enquirers used the lost email address, getting no response. Then they would go off in a huff and enquire elsewhere about accommodation, in the process, castigating people like me who don't bother answering their emails.

Then, out of the blue, 24 days into the saga, came the call from BT! They were going to reinstate my email address, *exactly* as it was. Now, this minute. Not in 100 days, but now! My Indian friend was all assurances, patience and good nature as he went about the business of resetting my account. All completed, I told him he had made my day, we exchanged pleasantries and bade each other a fond farewell, after checking it worked. I now had back my reliable Internet Explorer web browser, which they had previously exchanged for Firefox. Much though I loved that cheeky little fox, he was capricious in his dealings with me, playing a now-we-connect-you, now-we-don't game, which did not fit my mood. Now I have both the wilful fox and Internet Explorer. What fun! Or so I thought!

My journey to the Post Office was made reluctantly, with plenty to do preparing for our big celebration dinner that evening. The Postmaster appeared highly amused, making sure I couldn't see the front of the envelope I had to pay the surcharge on. It certainly was not a publisher's parcel of galley proofs with under-estimated postage, as I had been expecting.

'You're going to love this,' he grinned.

'Until I know what it is, I don't want it, never mind love it!' I snapped back.

'You will want it, when you know who it's from,' he said with obvious delight. Now I was hooked. I sneaked a look over the top of the envelope. My mouth dropped open. It had the British Telecom logo proudly displayed, but no franking! James was aware of my contretemps with BT, discussed at the time I posted the Recorded Delivery letter to their Chairman and it amused him highly that I should receive a letter back with no postage paid. I somehow think there is some rivalry between the skills of British Telecom and the skills of the Post Office, but I may be wrong.

'Would you like to pay me to get your letter from BT, then?'

In my best Queen Victoria voice, I righteously declared, 'We are not amused at having to pay to collect our mail!'

'I am,' he quipped! BT had certainly made his day.

Exiting the shop-cum-Post Office, money duly paid, receipt and letter firmly grasped, I glanced back, just to see if our esteemed Postmaster was still laughing like a drain. He was. I would remove him from my Christmas card list when I got home. No more gooey shortbread for him either.

Would you believe, what I paid to receive was the reply from no less a personage than Sir Christopher Bland, the Chairman of British Telecommunications, a mere few lines of acknowledgement to my letter, with the promise they would look into the matter! I wonder if his promise is more reliable than the Eastern promises of the last few weeks.

Things were tough at BT when even he could not afford a stamp, and here am I, expecting to be compensated for all the business they so carelessly lost me. Was this more evidence of their inability? Or maybe just adding insult to injury, just for the craic. I could conclude what I liked, and debated whether to laugh or cry. Good job I chose laughter because BT gave me the opportunity to cry later in the day.

About three times a day I usually nip into the office and check the emails. All had been well in the morning, happy to have my account back, I never gave a thought other than relief at no longer having this nagging anxiety, wondering who next was going to attack me for my unresponsive and irresponsible behaviour.

I do hope, genuinely, that this saga is not getting too tedious for you. I would hate to bore anyone with the inadequacies of monstrously large companies who make monstrously large profits, and are monstrously negligent in serving the needs of their poor little customers, totally at their mercy. Remember, I couldn't change my server because I needed that exact email address to continue taking in business from it so I had to stick it out with BT. Then their sudden capitulation and reinstating of my email account lifted my spirits to such joyous proportions, I was prepared to forgive all.

Even being told by my Indian friends that the hundreds of emails which would have been sent in the 24 days the account was closed were now lost in cyberspace did not dampen my relief that all was well again. What is lost is lost and there is nothing I can do about it was the most sensible attitude – cropping up again, isn't it – to take for my sanity, though I am concerned that a couple of my director-ships sometimes have sensitive material arriving by email. I did have a few qualms about that but BT said, 'Do not worry, Madam. I can assure you that nothing would be delivered to any other address. We are unable to access the emails so no one else can.' Did such assurances instil confidence? Em, I hate to say it, but no.

At lunch time, before I threw myself into preparations for the celebration that evening, I went to open my emails, feeling in fine good humour.

Open-mouthed disbelief as I stared at the screen! I wasn't even allowed on to the internet. No way. You have no internet connection I was blithely informed by my PC. Whose side was *it* on, then!

Nothing appeared wrong with my set up, no electrical blips. Pooh had not nipped into the office and switched off wireless, just for a wee laugh. The BT hub had one light going, so there was life in it, but there should have been a row of flashing lights to greet my request to get on the net. I had never seen this message before, that my network server did not *recognise* my address and if I wanted on to the internet, I must contact them. Contact BT!

Oh, hell. Not again! So I set about blowing my own fuse. The cats took off. Himself pleaded a trip to the wine cellar (the shed) to check out wines for dinner. Rebooting made no impression, but had I the opportunity to boot BT, I would have felt a million times better. I strongly suspected they were behind this new torment. There was no time to dally with them, trips to India being out of the question with so much to do. The unpaid postage had been a bit of a giggle, that they could be so inordinately stupid to respond to such a serious complaint with characteristic carelessness. But this was no laughing matter. It was worse than back to square one. No internet connection, nor could I think why, other than BT must have pulled the plug. The rotten toe rags!

I closed the office door and got on with the dinner, but niggling at the back of my mind was the thought that I was now in a worse position than ever and would never fill the empty spaces so I could end my career in B&B with as good a season as always. This was supposed to be the best of times, not the worst of times, both in terms of financial reward and pleasure, especially the last three-month run-down to the end of this final season. I had been looking forward to it for 40 years! With a house to build and plans laid, though no income secured other than what would come in through the business this year, I had reason to worry. Not a happy situation. So I abandoned the house and took to the hills with the dog.

We don't have a dog. Our cats would not like it, not one bit. I would like it, having had a dog for 13 years, but Himself would probably leave home at the prospect of harbouring more of my independently-minded four-legged friends, and then I would be seriously understaffed. But our little family over the road, fondly known as 'the tribe', have a dog, a lovely Chocolate Labrador, earnestly chosen as being the correct type to have around children, purported to have low brain density. Actually, she is very clever; the usual animal intelligence, able to easily understand what suits their purpose and very dim at realising your intent when it does not coincide with their needs. I wish I could achieve that appealing look of utter confusion coupled with such eager-to-please body language so my disobedience would be put down to nothing other than poor communications. I should practice more. Actually, the French are very good at it, Gallic charm delivered with many slow shoulder shrugs and little pouting 'poufs!' letting them off with whatever they don't want to do. Clever!

Shane had to wait until his eighth birthday for the much wanted dog. He was so uptight about its imminent arrival, he had to be sent home from school, physically sick with excitement. His two year old sister was also totally wound up awaiting the arrival of this puppy. Neil and Katrina had set off early in the morning to pick up the 16 week old animal, leaving the children annoyed to be stuck with Granny instead of the excitement of going for the puppy.

Their original choice of pup was to come from a litter that had, sadly, died at birth and when told there was another pup available in Aberdeenshire, but already named, Katrina was charmed to hear that her name was Molly. As a baby, Shane's comforter was a silky pair of pyjamas worn by his mother whilst nursing him in his first months. He dragged the bottoms everywhere and fondly called them his 'Molly'. Why, was a mystery, but he loved his Molly and could not be parted from the remnants until he was four! Not only that, Katrina teaches music and the proper name of this pedigreed pup included Allegro! It was fate. Molly must be theirs – ours, when it suits, though the cats vehemently disassociate themselves from such dubious ownership.

After spending a good few hours with Molly and her siblings, meeting the mother and owners, taking Molly to her own vet for a thorough check up, Neil continued on to his work on the oil rigs and Katrina set off on the long drive back, with Molly on board. Excitement mounted at home as I tried to keep the children calm. Then chaos when the puppy arrived. Shane was ecstatic and two year old Fallon seemed just as enthralled, although, in truth, until its arrival she wasn't really sure that the much wanted puppy was a living, and very lively, dog.

We believed all the cats, avid dog-haters, to be out but suddenly I spotted The Hobbit, on the highest point in the kitchen, perched on top of a cupboard glaring down at the puppy, ears pinned back and large eyes blazing. The minute Fallon saw the cat, she sped underneath the cupboard and earnestly entreated, 'Come down here Hobbit and bite the puppy!'

So, the puppy was not as welcome as we thought by this little girl who was the apple of her big brother's eye…until now. To her great chagrin, Hobbit did not come down and bite the puppy, so I picked her up and rocked her in my arms, settling into one of the big leather chairs in the kitchen. She seemed quite mollified until she looked round and saw her Papa, her own special Papa, gently stroking the head of the puppy.

Her tired little face crumpled as she looked up at me, her big blue eyes pools of misery. Very quietly, but quite emphatically, she opened a quivering mouth and said, 'Fucking puppy!'

We never heard her say it before, nor have we since. Of course, big brother got the blame, but I suspect it was from an older mouth she heard the profanity and noted the satisfaction it gave when things were not going well. You can imagine what the poor little dog was called, quietly mouthed, every time she put a paw wrong. She is now well over a year old and a boon to Fallon who blames her for every misdemeanour, even down to drinking all the spray polish when the little madam empties a tin in her efforts to help Granny with her work. 'Molly drank it all.' A lost watch. 'Molly ate it.' Coloured pen where it shouldn't be. 'Molly did it.' Book torn but no teeth marks. 'Molly chewed it. Her did! I saw her.'

I returned from a sprint through the hill with Molly and in much better form. Next day with the frivolities of the dinner party behind me – a fantastic time, anxieties duly dispensed with the help of some very good champagne and fine wines, kindly supplied by Bill and family – and with work settled for the day, I steeled myself to make that call to India, expecting the worst.

Twenty minutes later, as quick as that, well, relative to previous experiences, I put down the phone, glowing. I was back online, assured they had done nothing untoward, 'Madam, I can assure you, BT would not do that.' Although we went into this in a very convoluted way, all I had to do was unplug the hub connector, give it a wee rest, reinsert and wait a while, during which time we amicably chatted, about India, Scotland, the weather, as you do. Nothing happened and I was about to suggest a reviving brandy – for me, not the hub – when there it was, all lights flashing, and all systems go!

'What was the problem?' I earnestly enquired, all thoughts of reviving brandy gone.

'Madam, the hub required refreshing.' What a relief. Maybe a brandy would have helped its flagging energies after all. Anyway, it was at that point I could see why those poor incarcerated victims felt gratitude, bordering on love, towards their captors.

It was only afterwards doubt crept in and I suspiciously wondered why the hub had never required refreshing before, and why pick that particular day to lay down sticks and refuse to work anymore? But then, it is a BT hub, and could feel duty bound to help them when one of their customers goes as far as to start legal proceedings against them.

At this very moment, I'm casting suspicious glances in the hub's direction, eyeing up its green lights, waiting for them to go out, one by one, just to keep me under their control.

Notwithstanding the trauma with BT, it was a fantastic first to have Bill and the family stay, pure pleasure, giving wonderful memories. Malcolm, the oldest lad, now a solicitor, gave me some valuable advice should I go to law, so that hub just better transfer its loyalty to the person who paid for it. We shall have no more lying down on the job, waiting to be refreshed. Many a time I felt like that, but had to go on.

Other firsts have not been quite so good as I reflect, reminding me of why I am looking forward to my freedom.

'You have a room free, with a view, yes?', the heavily accented voice wafted over the line, to which I agreed, yes we had, offering the double bedded. 'We need a room with two beds. It is possible? Yes?'

Mmmmm, I thought quickly checking the register and noting that the people booked into the twin were well-known to me and would be just as happy in the double next door, both en suite, both over-looking the Bay, one a twin, the other with King size bed. I could make a swap for this Frenchman.

When they arrived, they were ever so nice, complimentary about the standards of cleanliness, she believing the house to be new! We had only the two couples staying and they got on well when intro-duced over tea and cakes late that afternoon.

I set the large dining table at the view end for the four of them, as I always did, doubling up on certain items though not the large condiment set, plates of home-made bread, others of fruit breads, another with scones and pancakes, all meant to be shared.

Next morning, the Continentals arrived in the dining-room first and after I greeted them, they helped themselves to fresh fruit, juices etc, whilst I headed back to do the final touches of cooking.

Arriving back to serve their coffee, I could hardly believe my eyes. They had moved the place setting away to the other end of the long table, virtually isolating themselves from my very hospitable English couple who had actually given up their twin room so their French cousins could have their view and separate beds! They took with them, to their side of the table, as much of the ingredients as they felt they would require. Oh, well, I thought. Each to their own and discreetly ensured my other couple had everything needed. Maybe they had all fallen out last night and I never twigged. Then, throughout the entire breakfast, they proceeded to chat across the divide like old friends.

'We thought you had separated us and did wonder why,' the bemused English couple laughed after the French left the dining room. They had stayed before and were rather puzzled at my unusual reorganisation for eating.

When I went to Madam and Monsieur's room after their departure, the furniture had been rearranged to allow the twin beds – and they had heavy wooden Sealy frames so shifting was no easy matter – to be pulled together. So much for the separate beds! Better still, the beautiful view so necessary to their stay was firmly shut out by the drawn curtains and pulled down blind, obliterating the panorama before them until their departure as near to 11 o'clock as possible! As I drew back the curtains and lifted the blind, pondering on their weird behaviour, the vision I looked out on could hold your attention for hours. So many people, my mother in particular, used to wonder how I could ever do any work with the distraction of such a view. I often wondered myself! But then, wondering at myself vied with wondering at the guests and here was reason to wonder.

Beds drawn together had happened before, as had the insistence upon a room with a view and the curtains firmly shutting out the view, but never a rearrangement of the breakfast table so a couple could dine separated from company, company they were happy to chat with during the evening and chatter amicably with during the whole breakfast service.

Yet I get asked, time and time again, which do I think is better, separate tables or a communal table. It depends on what you do really.

A communal table must be large enough to be thoroughly comfortable without encroaching on other people's space. It must be laid with sufficient generosity that none may feel they are preventing another from having as much as they fancy when taking from any communal plates. Generally speaking, your compliment of guests must enjoy breakfasting at an agreed convivial time in the morning, although you have to have the facility to serve separately if needs must. I discovered that 8.15am was a perfect time, those opting for 8.00am slipping in early, those preferring 8.30am arriving that bit later but making little difference to the congeniality of the table. Others of course wanted breakfast much earlier, to catch ferries or get a head start on the day, but very few wanted long lie ins.

In all honesty, I think the tendency is moving towards separate tables, with guests seldom meeting until they can view their fellow guests from a distance during breakfast, and that may suit some proprietors as well as it suits some guests. However, had that been the way I ran The Sheiling, we would never have had the fun, the repeat visitors or the tremendous get-togethers that occurred each June – and at several other times during the season. Various couples met up, often no less than five couples congregated round that communal table to catch up on a year's living and added gusto to my job satisfaction and excitable prospects to my coffers, but boy, was it hard work!

12

Things We Do For Our Guests

NEWLY RETURNED FROM a journey even more dangerous than venturing into our kitchen in the morning when breakfast is in full swing, one look at me and you may be forgiven for thinking I have a space ship out back, ready to hop into: heavily booted, boiler suited, suspiciously hooded, gloved up and face masked, missing only the breathing apparatus and believe me, had I such a contraption, I would be wearing that too. Then I would have avoided swallowing those flies in an involuntary gasp of air when I pitched to the ground before remembering there was a midge mask in my pocket. It proved to be quite ineffective, allowing kamikaze midges to follow the flight of the fly. At least I wouldn't have to bother eating dinner tonight! And no, I was not out persuading honey bees to allow me into their hive. We don't have domestic bees and see fewer and fewer wild bees as the years go by, no matter the masses of flowers to attract them.

It was one of those rare sunny afternoons 2007 saw fit to bestow upon us and I prayed no one would ring the doorbell as I collapsed into a perspiring heap in the kitchen eager to view my spoils.

'Mmmmm! Not near so good as last year, much more difficult to come by too,' I complained, Himself not in the least surprised to see me stagger in looking like something from outer space.

I could have had more if I had stuck to my carefully planned assault course instead of letting confidence overwhelm me, just at the very last, thinking how well I was doing, turning for home unscathed.

Last year, in glorious sunshine, Katrina and the children came down from the hill ground sporting boxes of the most delicious looking wild raspberries. This was the very next day after I came up from Balvraid Farm where I annually spent hours, en route back from meetings in Inverness, tired and fractious, fielding midges, stuffing what room is left in the car with trays of the raspberries we use for the rest of the season. We freeze them for Christmas and for the start of the next season, their popularity making the tremendous effort of hand picking at least 24 punnets worth the inevitable angst. And so well it should, considering their cost! But by braving the midges in the balmy evenings and forgetting it would be midnight by the time I got home with all the fruit and a car full of goodies to sort out, and the ironing (how could I ever forget the ironing that no other would undertake in my absence) by picking them myself, I knew I would have a perfect product for freezing. I could also sustain my energy levels by intermixing the fly and midge diet with surreptitiously swallowing a few raspberries. Balvraid grew a fantastic berry for the freezer, but, if you put a dish of those out against a dish of tatty looking small produce off the hill, it is the hill fruit the guests go for. Local, you see. That is what matters to the discerning visitor and the hill rasps did have a taste that belied their stunted looks!

Imagine me not being aware there was a hill full of the most expensive of soft fruits right in front of me, and at no cost. Or so I thought! The marketing potential of local produce was the real lure though, so, well warned to put on long trousers to avoid scratches from wild undergrowth on bare legs, off I set. In comparison with other hazards, like BT, ever ready to thwart me – there's been more but I won't upset myself by detailing further altercations at this time – scratch attacks seemed honest and harmless.

On our land you now have to be extremely careful where you put your feet but of this I was well aware, having ventured off the beaten pathways shortly after our son took over most of the land. In an endeavour to avoid having anything to do with the vagaries of animal husbandry, keenly remembering my debacles to keep the croft in working order, he planted no less than 13,000 native trees. The scheme was greatly encouraged by the Forestry Commission and almost sabotaged by a B&B couple who thought we must have been going to make money out of it, or use it for some tourism project that may give us an edge in attracting custom! Can't think of any other reason for such strenuous opposition to so sensible a scheme, even to the extent of lobbying neighbours to try and get someone to find a valid objection.

That backfired as no neighbour objected, with the chap next door to us taking a delight in telling us he was plead with to stop the trees being planted, and astounded our adversaries by saying, on the contrary, he was very happy to assist Neil by accepting the contract to do all the necessary deer and rabbit fencing! I would love to have seen their faces, but that kind of satisfaction is never yours to make up for the hassle and hard work such determined, and totally unnecessary, harassment causes. As it is, rather than make money, implementing such a scheme on a North Coast croft requires deep pockets and extensive energy to ensure good annual growth, maintenance of access pathways almost requiring the skills of a forest ranger. Each tree had to be planted on a large divot of earth that left in its wake a death-trap hole, if you don't look where you're going.

In time this hole filled with water. That was fine. Indeed, that was the desired effect, to ensure the rooting tree had plenty moisture to keep it going. You saw the little pools where only an idiot would step, though surprising how many idiots there are out there, me included. Getting down on your knees and peering into their murky depth drew gasps of amazement at the wild life they attracted, this becoming one of Shane's favourite haunts, especially during tadpole time, water-spider watching and newt hunting expeditions. However, as the years passed, those holes became camouflaged with grass, weeds, flowers, even tiny seedlings of new trees. Innocently stepping onto another piece of perceived safe ground, suddenly, like Alice In Wonderland, down the hole you went, lucky not to break an ankle. It made you very conscious of where to put your feet and of course, the best raspberries were in the most inaccessible places, surrounded by holes, rocks, stones and nettles, not to mention the rapidly returning whins Neil had spent years of his time digging out. New growth from old roots is impossible to deter so when you do fall, it's not a good idea to throw out your palms to save your fall, much better to plonk down on your backside making the wearing of canvas padded trousers almost mandatory! Heavy industrial gloves are great but must come off when picking the fruit and that's a prime time to take a tumble.

To stay safe, all that is required is the ability to balance oneself whilst putting a foot down tentatively, ready to pull back when met with no resistance on this dangerously uneven ground. If error is made, fall easily, not fighting it, because down you are going to go anyway. The art of falling comes easy to me after years of being turfed off Bronco's back, with him cute enough to ensure I was pitched into soggy wet ground or patches of nettles, if there were no hard punishing sand in the vicinity of his revolt. He knew where every nettle grew on the land and took a delight in digging up the roots which he would assiduously clean on the stone walls, jealously guarding his pile of the white, fibrous goodies, then happily munch away at this little cache. He offered an occasional piece to Troubie, who was not into this soporific delicacy that made Bronco's eyes roll and sent him into a mystic trance. I would love to have tried it myself but was never offered any. Eventually he ridded the entire croft of nettles, no mean task, but now, with the horses long gone to their land beyond these green fields, those stinging weeds are well and truly back.

The raspberries are new though, making their first appearance last year and in reasonable abundance. They grew in profusion since the land no longer had sheep or horses to stem such growth, but this year their fruit crop was very poor, akin to the apples and other fruits and berries that usually grew so well. Still, I was determined to gather a tasty bite for my very special guests, Bill, Joan and their family, hence the get-up and the state of collapse.

Despite the fruit being so small, it surprised and pleased how the basket began to fill, aiding the temptation to go deeper into the undergrowth when tiny glints of bright red drew the eye to yet another possibility of more fruit hidden in treacherous terrain.

Intact, no accident to mar my afternoon of careful stealth and heading for home, I spotted a few beauties ahead and took a step without looking. Down I went, nettles, whins, fruit flying, wild curses competing with the distinctive calls of a pair of mating curlews, the first we had seen on the land in years. How long would they stay with us, I pondered as I lay looking skywards, bemoaning my carelessness and praying for the strength to gather my scattered spoils.

Avoiding further mishap and with the remains of my afternoon's work firmly grasped, I made my way back to the inevitable collapse, wondering if our guests were ever aware of the lengths to which some of us go, just to please.

'Where on earth have you been?' Himself had the temerity to ask when I returned from one particular shopping expedition, uptight, tummy rumbling ominously, there being no time to eat, temper frayed and ready to unravel, hair sticking out all over the place and eyes glassy with concentration. I sourced the goods by tearing round every shop in the vicinity, determined to buy only the best for my precious guests, avoiding casual meetings, there being no time to stop and chat, then drove the forty miles home. Such were my needs that the closest town of Thurso would not suffice, so every now and again I ventured into the county capital of Wick to ensure a fully ticked shopping list. If I'd had the presence of mind to pick the list off the table top before I left in my usual flurry. This omission merely added to the spoils in the belief that if I bought everything, then what was written out so assiduously would be satisfied by a full compliment of groceries. That marathon behind me, I collapsed into a chair thinking only of food for myself. It took a minute to realise I was being ticked off for my tardiness!

'The people arrived hours ago and they wanted to see you,' I was scolded. 'I said you would be back long before now,' delivered with just enough edge of crabbiness to grab my full attention. He took in the wild look in my eyes and gaping mouth preparing for a torrent of defence but I didn't have the energy and this man, who knew me well, was wise enough to err on the side of caution, quietly adding, 'You'll be hungry.'

'Which ones?' I sighed, sinking into the depth of the comfortable leather chair and sniffing the air for signs of appeasing that gnawing hunger.

'The ones you told to come any time and you would sort out their itinerary. The Americans. The others phoned and it could be midnight before they arrive.'

Oh, god! Midnight! That was a stinker, having got up at the crack of dawn, before 5.30am, to see a couple off on the all-day Orkney Trip, well fed and watered. 'Oh, yes, come along any time. We'll be pleased to see you and you can be sure the kettle will be on,' I blithely conveyed, hospitality oozing out of every pore, never thinking that anytime could be 11 or 12 o'clock at night. Eleven am or 12 noon would be fine by us. We're delighted to have guests enjoy the comfort and relaxation we offer so their stay is lengthened, if only by a few hours, rather than rush in late and leave early next day. It means too that the tea, coffee and home bakes ritual is over and done with at a decent time of day.

'You would have given them tea,' I said, more concerned about the offer of scheduling their timetable, usually a long and arduous task. This had started in one of the many email enquiries that heralded their stay and continued on until arrival, when they would have me as their captive tourist information officer on a one-to-one basis with no queue of impatient visitors heckling from behind.

At least these Americans wanted to sort this out at the beginning of what was only a one night stay. The American propensity to rush around Scotland in a day put us all under pressure trying to help them out with their impossible schedules. Impatience was hidden with that ever-present smile, from the couples who had all evening to ask their inevitable list of questions whilst I floated about tending their needs, giving the impression of having time only for them, quality time. Then in the morning, after breakfast when I'm trying to field phone calls, get the perishable goods off the table and into the fridge, put through credit cards, make yoghurt, mentally tick off all that has to be seen to in the house, plus all the rest before new guests arrive, nothing will be done on time because I will be wearing my information officer hat. How often, during an evening, when I've implored guests to allow me to give them all the information necessary to continue with their journey tomorrow do they dismiss me with, 'Oh, let's leave it until the morning when we're more in the mood!' The British are not too bad at this as they have a sensitive side that picks up the fact you are there and willing now, and the mornings are fairly busy. But the Americans! Sensitivity to anything other than their schedule is not high on their agenda.

With all this going on in the home front, it became more and more difficult to maintain the agency work that had gathered in momentum as I got to grips with my solid belief that here, in the Northern Highlands, my beloved Sutherland had an abundance of the best of experiences to offer. Along with her sister and neighbouring counties of Ross-shire and Caithness, I believe there are extremes of the very best of opportunities but, to get the information out there, it required many in the trade – and some admirable people who were not in the trade – to work behind the scenes. I was one of those stalwart people, wearing so many different hats, if I stopped to look in a mirror, I may well recognise the hat, but at times I was hard pushed to recognise the person beneath the millinery that was beginning to dominate my life.

As to the wearing of many hats, I had a colleague Himself used to refer to as 'Her of the Many Hats!' after she kept contacting me saying, 'Now, with my Visitor Guide hat on today, could you tell…' and so it would go on through the many jobs she valiantly fielded. There was a while when my own hats spilled out from the coat cupboard, into the office, climbed the stairs into our bedroom and all over the place. I've since managed to divest most with good grace, though one I had to eat, and another my head got too big for. So a rather possessive colleague threw at me in a spiteful email when a journalist did not include her name in an article after I had painstakingly given all her contact details for that purpose, knowing what she was like. Being involved in journalism myself, I know how unreliable we can be when others try to write our articles for us. 'Yes, of course, we'll include that,' then go off and file the completed copy, looking good and missing out what an editor would see as unnecessary script, and quite right too. But, when an ego is dented, sparks can fly!

'Don't lose any sleep over someone like that' was Himself's only comment yet the grin on his face betrayed his relief that a rather demanding person he particularly disliked would now be out of my life. Time and time again, when I would persevere with a so-called friendship, his opinion, which I would set aside with misplaced loyalty, would prove correct in the long run.

The hat eating episode came from curling up in a ball one night and saying mournfully as I shuffled mounds of paperwork, 'If I'm still a member on this board by the end of the season, I'll eat my hat!' I was, but I didn't eat the hat. It was too heavy with due diligence and financial acumen giving severe bouts of indigestion. Little did I realise that when I gleefully stepped down, I would end up accepting their offer of employment, throwing my so-called retirement plans to the winds.

I went from the frying-pan into the fire when I escaped secretarial work to do B&B. What in the name of goodness was I thinking of when I went from the fire into a sizzling chip pan, but that tale is not for this book.

It was hard finding the stamina to attend such brain-draining meetings, then please my guests by heading off to buy fresh produce to ensure my table lived up to the promise that may well have enticed visitors to stay in the first place, then come home at midnight and do the ironing so they could slip into freshly laundered sheets. Some of us operators did outstanding favours for guests, taking them out on runs to see sunsets, taking them here, there and everywhere, shopping for them, plying them with drink, partying with them, putting on entertainment for them, nice surprises in bedrooms when anniversaries were announced, use of telephones, soup and sandwiches with the inevitable coffee and cakes offered time and time again when arriving late and not managing to source their own meal, all free gratis. Washing fly-spotted windscreens to greet them as they prepare to drive away (one friend in the business thinking nothing of doing the whole car). Then there's dishing out home-made goodies to take back with them, doing their washing and ironing, sitting up late with them listening to all sorts of fascinating stories. It is all worth it when you hear pleasure in the voice as a particularly pleasant evening is recounted with the best of local food and you salivate as they recall every morsel.

Sometimes though, an act of kindness can get you into serious trouble, like years ago, when we had our horses. They were an attractive and very friendly pair. Troubie was a rich chestnut coloured 14.2hh part Arab, spirited and quite devoted to his bossy stable-mate, Bronco, a 16.2hh Dunn, part thoroughbred/part mad, gelding with a devious mind. I rode a lot then and the horses were in tip-top condition, keen on getting out and used to doing a bit of hacking and trekking with my horsy friends, who at that time ran a stable a comfortable hack from our home. But their place was closed when a young French couple booked in with me, eyed up our equines and moaned that they had come to Scotland hoping to get great horse-riding but were disappointed. I explained we never hired our horses, we were uninsured, and they belonged to my son and me, not for the use of guests. It was a best ignored, oft made plea to ride such fine animals, but the risk was not worth taking as Bronco was capable of proving his rider much less competent than they had me believe. It was a lesson he took unmitigated pleasure in drumming into my battered body as I slowly learned how to outwit him.

Next day, doing their room, the expensive riding kit hanging unused gave me a huge twinge of conscience on behalf of the poor horse riding opportunities my country had offered then. What a shame, I thought, while making the beds, gullible to the last. They must be very experienced riders. I was going for a day out with my mother, and there, in the field were two horses gasping to get out for a good long hack with competent equestrians. Gasping to get out for a good long laugh, more like, but sometimes my impulsive gestures did not foresee other than the joy on the face when I would magnanimously agree to some hair-brained idea.

I explained the risk was their own, no payment, but they were welcome to exercise the horses, the tack hung up in the barn next to the stable, the head collars to bring in the horses were there as well. But instead of taking the horses to the stable to tack up, they said they would tack them in the front park where they were peacefully grazing: innocence on four legs.

I left them to it after hauling out all the gear into the field while they disappeared. They reappeared, kitted out fit to put a dressage Olympic contestant in the shade reminding me I should get into more interesting kit myself. My mother duly arrived, consternation written all over her face, 'What's going on with the horses in the park below the house?'

'Oh, we have riders in and they're going to take them out.' I grabbed my car keys, wondering where on earth I had put the shopping list this time and glanced out the window.

'Oh, well you know best yourself.' My mother's diplomatic reminder I should stop and think should have been fair warning. Bronco and Troubie were standing intently watching the guests. The guests were walking round, and round, and round, staring at the ground where I could see the saddles lying. 'Are you all right?' I shouted, puzzled.

'Meybe.' He gave a Gallic shrug. 'We are not zo sure. Thees ees meybe a leetle deeferent, ze tack!'

It never occurred to me to go back to the house and change my heels, thinking this would be just a little hiccup, something a tiptoe into the park would soon sort out. The scene that met me when I opened the gate was jaw dropping! I had left each bridle on the gate, ready to slip over the horses' heads with only the main straps to fasten. Now the leathers lay, spread out on the ground as if for cleaning, in all their separate little pieces. Every single piece had been unbuckled and slipped out of leather keepers, even the bits were unbuckled. It looked like a manual of how to put a bridle together! The belly bands were separated from the saddles and the stirrups neatly laid out, detached from their leathers, of course.

No wonder Bronco and Troubie were fascinated. 'That is normal tack. Why did you take it all to pieces?' I was more puzzled than annoyed.

'Eet ees zo deeferent, Madam. We are 'appy to have ze mounts ready to step into ze saddle,' and all I thought was, boy, they really are well off, grooms, as well as the most expensive riding gear I had ever set eyes on. My own boots, an indulgence, were hand-made in Germany but you should have seen theirs! I just wished it were my boots on my feet and not smart town shoes sinking into the grass as I set about repairing the damage.

It would take me ages to sort that lot out and by now Bronco was thumping me on the back with his head, a habit brought on by his intention to persuade me to giddy-up while the notion was on him to go places. He was certain it had the same effect on me as a knee-squeeze had on him when I wanted a bit more action. Trying to keep my balance and my heels from sinking further into the turf as well as the smile fixed on my face was tough and each time I glanced up, my mother's impatience grew more evident.

'Go in and make tea. I think I may be a while,' I warned, wondering if I should give in and go and take off the tight skirt and heels, but eventually, me dirty and sweating, the excited pair – the guests, not the horses who were behaving rather suspiciously well – immaculate, not a hair out of place as they sprung like veterans into the saddles. That came as a relief after their tacking-up inability, nevertheless, I was a bit sceptical of Bronco as he could play up something wicked. The French chap held him on a fairly tight rein, which the horse liked, pulling in his head and picking up his feet into a showy trot. Troubie, who was our son's pony, would be fine. His wife was just the right size for him and they made a lovely picture as I opened the gate, gave explicit instructions how to access, through our fields on the other side of the main road, the inviting looking riverside, then the beach and the open hills.

By the time I reached the house to clean my shoes, my face, my hands and remove the spittle Bronco had left when cleaning his nose on my back, they had turned into the first of the fields below the road. They could certainly sit well in the saddle and had trotted the horses down the main road, stopping to open the gate and get back on board without mishap. The fact Bronco was behaving impeccably should have been a warning. He hadn't put a hoof out of place which was so unlike him. He could be wilful to a fault and was a known character in the village. He loved his pint and it took determination and skill to get him past the pub on the two mile ride round the village we often enjoyed, and often did not, dependent upon his antics en route. I enjoyed it when I got my way; he enjoyed it when he got his way. But we loved each other. No doubt in either of our minds about that.

My brother, Neil, on some of his trips home from sea would take him out and vowed the horse would not pass the pub so they both had to have a couple of pints, or so, before coming straight back home! He would then tell me that once Bronco got his pint, no way was he going further, a full turn around and home at the gallop! Contrary to our trips out, Neil and Bronco *always* enjoyed their outings together!

I watched anxiously as the Frenchman took the lead. The horses knew the way to the beach with their eyes closed, going there several times a week. But when their riders got them under way, Bronco set off in the opposite direction. I had explained exactly where to go and expected him to be turned to the correct route, immediately! Instead, the four-legged reprobate picked up a bit of pace and quickly took his French rider through into the hayfield, a strictly forbidden area. Troubie swung in after him, furtively looking to right and left then back over his shoulder to check if his rider was going along with this interesting diversion. Troubie was not inclined to initiate insubordination but happily went along with all of Bronco's escapades, and there were many. We took on Troupa D'Or of Melvich, to give him his registered title, as a foal of nine months, and at the time of this incident we'd had him for six fascinating years. Bronco had been with us all of four years, a spirited eight-year-old now who never let Troubie forget, he was two years the senior and must be obeyed!

They were too far away to go racing after them in my clobber as Bronco was now fair spanking it out, cutting a fine swathe through the nicely matured hay, patiently waiting for the attentions of the mower. What a blessing Himself was on the rig! There was another field where they were heading which could take them out onto the riverside. But no, Bronco, having reached the foot of the hayfield now swung round and broke into a standing-start gallop, preceded by a leap that matched the one my heart gave. I was no longer worrying about the hay, eyes glued to the guests I was responsible for, as their mounts careered up the field, manes flying and riders clinging on.

I drove the car to the top of the road, intent on telling them to take the horses back home and abandon what had been a very bad idea anyway. They flew past me and cantered on towards the beach, on the correct path this time, not a path made for cantering for fear of rabbit holes and the undulating stony ground. We watched, my mother demanding to know if I had lost my senses, letting people like that have the horses, me praying for their safety when suddenly they disappeared into a gully, a difficult fern covered area the horses were never ridden into. After a while we saw them head out onto the riverside through a completely different gate to the one I always used, not heading for the beach as I assumed. There was a good river crossing, the only one we ever used for safety of depth and to protect the water pipes laid on the river bed, taking fresh water to Bighouse. By now I wasn't surprised to see the horses saunter past this natural ford, heading off up river. I raked for the binoculars lying in the car. They were all a long way off by now.

There was no decent hacking in that direction, but there was a reason for going there. My heart sank. It was here we took them for a fast gallop, on hard riverside sands. Bronco wouldn't, surely. Not with new riders who had no control whatsoever over his behaviour, the swing of his backside and proud lift of his head easily told who was in charge. If you did not rein in the horse at the end of the gallop, you were met with large stones and broken ground where a leg could easily be smashed, or a head! He was swift when he took off and very strong in the neck and shoulder, the only blessing being a soft mouth, but he had ways of conning an innocent rider into getting the bit between his teeth.

He stood at the top of the gallop, patiently waiting for Troubie to get in line. There was absolutely nothing I could do but pray! I never said a word to my mother who had already castigated me, now an hour behind schedule, for getting myself into such a pickle, 'And why?' she kept asking herself, me never daring to draw breath, leave alone answer.

That evil creature even allowed Troubie a head start! Oh, the scally-wag! What an incentive to go like hell, just to overtake his stable-mate, and Troubie was fleet enough of foot. It appeared all the plans belonged to Bronco and the end result would be in the lap of the gods. I desperately searched for something, anything I could offer to give up in exchange for their safety, for the ability of the riders to gain control and bring the animals to a planned stop before they all broke their necks. Chocolate! Nights out! No more new shoes, give away all my handbags, anything but I couldn't concentrate on personal sacrifice as my mind raced over the possibilities of how they would meet their fate.

If they didn't rein in, I knew what would happen. I'd been there, done that! Bronco was as fly as a fox as I had learned the hard way. Out that first summer, at the top of the gallops, having been turfed off once before, I had him under full control, no amiable chat while we moved quietly and sedately on, but it was a hot day and he was thirsty. Really, really thirsty. If I did not let him have a drink, he would die of thirst. He needed that drink now or he would never make it home. His head tossed and his foot kicked one of many pools of rain water scattered over the hard turf that edged that long length of firm river sands.

Cautiously, I leaned over his neck, for no way was I giving him a long loose rein. I'd been conned before by that one. This way, one tensing of his body for the off and I would have enough short rein to hold him in. He was totally relaxed as his nose touched the pool. He never as much as took a sip. His body bunched, I gasped and drew the reins in hard. But I did not have on my usual leather riding gloves, just silly non grip material that seemed perfectly sensible riding a perfectly sensible horse.

As the reins slipped through my fingers he clamped on the bit and we were off, pounding down the sands, gathering momentum with each length and heading straight for the stones. I couldn't bear the thought of him breaking his neck through my ignorance and his own fool-hardiness. I would break his neck later... if we survived. With no sign of getting him under any control, I used all my leg and seat strength to swerve his body towards the river. It worked, except he went that way and I went the other, a hard fall on the sands, knocking me out.

I came to, bleeding copiously from the mouth and the nose, thankful I still had my teeth. And where was my loving mount? Gone. Nowhere to be seen, no anxious standing over the body to see if it was dead, like you see in old romantic movies. Not a bit of it. No way was he waiting to take the blame for this fiasco. He could have got washed away in the river for all I cared as I limped for home, stemming the flow of blood and invective, the worst part knowing the fault was my own.

And there was the culprit, nonchalantly leaning over a gate leading into our land some distance from the gate we normally used. As I slowly made my way towards him, he made little burring, anxious whinnies, a look of utter sorrow across his long equine face. Why had I gone and fallen off like that in the middle of a good game? You could see he was at pains to understand me.

'You wicked, rotten, sod!' I screeched.

'Well, actually, a bee stung my bum and there could have been a whole swarm, so I had to get you out of trouble,' he gently whinnied back, the look of concern stemming my vocal attack as I tried to find an excuse for his performance.

There was no excuse. I had been well warned, that first spring he came to stay, when he egged Troubie into rounding up the newly born lambs, to play with, my new horse insisted; to kill, Himself decided, landing the pair of them a long expensive holiday at a correctional school on the Black Isle. Troubie proved a perfect pupil, Bronco defied them, earning himself the nickname, The Killer, and no one would ride him out. When I visited, they watched like a hawk as I rode a perfectly behaved mount. He couldn't be that bad, could he? He was a joy to sit on and made clear his horror that I was merely visiting and not taking him back home. When they did eventually come home, I was immediately punished by being studiously ignored while friends were fussed over, Himself too was treated as his saviour and the transport we used to take the horses away and bring them back could never be used again. Bronco adamantly refused to set foot in their horsebox again, despite hours and hours of trying, him ending up with a black eye so he could get the vet on his side, me ending up with a mortgage to pay the bills it all entailed. He won. We had to change our hirers much to Troubie's disgust, having been carted about by them since his very first show.

At the school they advised if I had a rapport with him, he *could* be okay, but they would never trust him, so he had no dedicated rider, like Troubie, to bring him under proper guidance.

I reminded him of this, and the fact that he had been en route to the knacker's yard when a young farmer was enticed by his looks and bought him on impulse. It was the farmer who engendered a taste for Tennant's Special in the wayward horse but when Bronco jumped fences to arrive at the pub without his rider, he had to go. I bought him as he recovered from a well stitched leg after his latest dash to the pub involved leaping a barbed-wire fence. When Himself and myself arrived to look at the horse, there was an air of tense silence when I trotted him gently round the field. After a couple of little bucks, he was brilliant and I fell totally in love with him, though he managed somehow to rip the pocket of Himself's good jacket, engendering a deep suspicion that something was not quite right though he could not put his finger on it. When I got my horse home, he took against Himself with a vengeance and would not allow him on his back. Not a good move, but time saw a truce which grew into reciprocal respect, mostly because I kept incidents like the mad gallops to myself, and Himself ensured he had a grape to hand when mucking out the stable until it became no longer necessary.

What his excuse would be for today's unbelievable misbehaviour with my guests I would never know because he would be dead, the guests probably too. There wasn't time to wonder about my public liability insurance or what else I could offer up in exchange for their safety when, quite suddenly, Bronco swerved away from the stones and went full tilt into the river, not the normal safe crossing but a deep flowing part.

I never got the chance to be thankful about not breaking their necks on the gallops because they would all drown now anyway and that would be worse because I wouldn't even have the bodies to send back to France, these tidal waters being ever so swift. Even my mother was out of the car and craning her neck at this development. It certainly stopped his speeding antics as he took the flow on his chest, almost half way across now. But what of poor Troubie? He would be swept away.

I shut my eyes. When I opened them that sensible animal was crossing by the ford and met Bronco hauling himself out of the water – his saddle, and his rider, dripping wet. Bronco loved water and had a penchant for throwing you into the sea which he thought a hilarious lark. I learned later, that trick of depositing his rider into the sea had added to the farmer's reasons to find him another mug, but not until I too had to swim ashore after my errant mount saw fit to take a dive into a big wave. As the waves covered us his huge body passed over my head, his mane swirling out behind him, his eyes wide open and he too looked shocked at the depth of water he had dived into. Thankfully he never did it again!

I watched now, weak with anticipation, as they sedately trotted up the Bighouse road and headed for the hills, where they should have been an hour before, had my horse behaved and the riders taken control.

We made a belated trip to town, fuelled by my anxiety, hoping upon return, the guests would be home and the horses back in the field. They were not. I spent what was left of the day wearing a path between kitchen and front window, until at last I saw them coming up the land, demurely trotting the proper pathway. Cooking abandoned, I rushed out to see what kind of state they were in. They'd had no food since breakfast and now it was coming up on five o'clock.

'Are you both OK?' I anxiously asked, absolutely terrified of the answer.

'We are zo good.' I was more shocked than pleasantly surprised to hear.

'Why didn't you take the path I indicated to the beach,' I implored, after ensuring all was well with the horses too, still waiting for their castigation for giving them a delinquent animal for a so-called pleasure ride.

'Oh, ze orse knew a better way,' said as if there was not a problem in the world.

'The orse,' said I, at my indignant best, though never quite managing to catch the eye of the said horse, 'is supposed to go where he is told!

You wouldn't allow your horses at home to do what they like, now would you?'

'Ah, Madam, we ave not got ze orses at ome. We go out, only from ze stables, with a group of peoples and orses. And the orses always know where to go. One orse, he follow ze other. It is good, Madam, yes.'

His young wife piped up then, looking at the tack with a puzzled frown, 'We ad the most fun ever. It was zo very good. He is a very good orse,' she added, patting Troubie's nose and walking off, leaving me to remove the puzzling tack, just as she did at the stables at home.

It should have been a salutary lesson in keeping such magnanimous gestures to myself, but of course, it wasn't. Never being one to learn a lesson from the first mistake, when a new, young and decidedly cocky policeman came to the village, arriving on my doorstep to say he was a keen rider and really fancied taking out Bronco my optimistic belief that he knew what he was doing ruled the day.

'Sure you can,' I heard myself saying, 'but he's not such an easy ride and is wilful,' I warned. With a pitying look in my direction, off they set for the beach, returning a couple of hours later, looking none the worse, until on getting closer I noticed loads of scratches all over the rider's bare arms. He assured me it was a great ride, great horse, easy peasy, and he would look forward to next time. Bronco glowed under the praise showered upon his glossy back, enjoying extra rations for being such a good boy.

Our constable never did come back and on my first ride to the beach the next day, I could see why. The beautiful golden sand of the long beach at Melvich is guarded by a very steep bank fringed by thickly growing, and sharply pointed, marram grass running into the sand dunes. Up and down the banks, interspersed every now and then with broken, scratchy grass, where some heavy load had been repeatedly dumped, were the hoof prints of a horse. I knew those hoof prints. Boy, I hoped I would require no favours from the law for the duration of our new copper's stay.

He was not the first policeman to suffer from Bronco's wayward-ness. It became the custom, after being shod, an experience Bronco did not particularly enjoy, to get telephone calls from anywhere in the village saying, 'Did you know your horses are running wild in Portskerra?' This was a mile away, and they could have been here, there, or anywhere except the field they had been left in.

One day I looked out the window in time to see the pair of them, sparks flying from their newly shod feet, tearing up the road. We had no idea how they always managed to get out from gates that had been securely tied. This time they could not be found anywhere and at midnight I gave up the search, as did friends who helped, and reluctantly we headed off for our various beds. Early next morning, Usdean, on his way to work called. He was laughing.

'Your two horses were in the policeman's garden, eating his cabbages, early this morning!'

Oh, nice one Bronco! Our friend had managed to get them out and put them in a nearby field and I got Neil up and off we went, shame-faced, to get the culprits home and make amends.

It was some time before we realised that Bronco could very easily untie, by working away quietly with his teeth, many different knots, Himself being a rigger and used to tying all kinds of loads securely, failing to outfox Bronco who went where he pleased during the long wait on the delivery of the delayed latches for the newly set up gates in most of the fields. What a relief when they were all secured, the springs so tight I cursed them almost as much as I cursed Bronco for his wicked, wayward, ways.

13

So That's It Then

MY HEART SANK as the tirade on the doorstep continued. This time it was not I who was the culprit, enacting bad attitude with 'Pride & Passion'. That project is going from strength to strength, testimony to this is on their website where all sorts of valuable information helpful to a trade member can easily be found. No, this time it was a legitimate guest. I had innocently, and in fair good humour, answered the bell, fully expecting new arrivals, their dinner now well prepared. Instead an elderly Australian man stood there, back to the door, admiring the view.

'Got a room?' he cut into my friendly greeting. 'Great view you have here.'

'I have one double left if you would like to see it,' usual smile at the ready though trying to weigh up this curt newcomer. After all, it's a very vulnerable occupation, taking under one's roof just about anyone who applied. You're duty bound to put up with all sorts of personalities, some of whom had it in for me before I opened my mouth because where they stayed the night before did not come up to expectations and they were not going to let that happen again! In the main, this grudging stance is a thing of the past, and the episode came with this Australian from the distant past. It still lingers in the memory, casting its long shadow of suspicion on all his countrymen, until they vindicate themselves through their own delightful personalities. The reverse happens then, when we greet with half-hearted enthusiasm, thinking, 'Oh, my god. Another Australian', instead of, 'How lovely to meet you,' just because the last Aussie had proved a joy to be rid of.

When we set foot upon foreign soil we ought to bear in mind that many will be judged in the light of how we ourselves behave. That's not the way it works though with few feeling the need to behave in case anyone thinks badly of their fellow countrymen and women. Frankly, the Australians in particular didn't give much of a damn, no more than we do when we British go abroad and act according to our natures, rather than at our best because we're English or Scottish, or indeed Welsh. As for being Irish, well, they seem to get off with just about anything, and we love them for it. At least most of us do!

'How much?' my Commonwealth cousin had barked. Australians, particularly the older types, did not waste time on the niceties as they searched out accommodation. Before the days of making acquaintances over the airways through websites gave the opportunity to arrive in a more congenial frame of mind that is. The virtual wanderings through premises and email communications, long before actual arrival, gives the modern day security in anticipation.

This man scrutinised me suspiciously, announcing a sceptical, 'I'll have a look!' Typical of this breed, his better half remained ensconced in the car with no say in the matter, admiring the view no doubt.

We had all five rooms on the go then, two upstairs, three down. Three of them overlooked the bay, the one I was about to show, over-looked a rather nice garden at the back with patios and seating beneath rolling hills and lots of blue sky. A belt of half-grown trees fringed a brae resplendent in a coat of golden gorse, interspersed with beautiful sprays of the paler yellow broom. I pushed the door to this room wide, allowing him to enter first.

'What about a front room with that bay view?'

'I'm sorry, all the other rooms are in use.'

He looked round what was a rather nice room, every piece of fur-niture made especially out of pale Russian Maple, to suit the room and the needs of guests and greatly admired by one of our Inspectors, who had been a cabinet maker. The soft furnishings were made by MacKenzie's with the window framed in a particularly lovely Swiss style, no frills, design with quality material in an off-white back-ground, with bright sprigs of spring flowers. I liked it. Others liked it. My would-be guest took the antipodean stance.

'What is wrong with you people?' he irritably demanded, hands raised in supplication to whatever god he believed in.

'Why? What's wrong with the room?' I asked, stepping back from his affronted gesticulations.

'There's nothing wrong with the room,' he looked exasperated, but refrained from adding 'you stupid woman'. 'But, why isn't it at the front? What is it with you people? You have the most wonderful views in this country and you build houses with rooms...' by now I was trotting after him as he stormed to the front door, '...that do not take advantage of *that* view!' He flung out his arms embracing all that lay before him, his provocation palpable.

'We have three bedrooms overlooking that bay, a lounge as well as a dining-room, all with *that* view' I countered, my own ire rising on behalf of the impossibility of building homes with every room looking out front. 'The room you were offered has a lovely outlook,' I defended, thinking of the many blank walls – and worse – I had looked out on in my travels.

'But they should all look out on *that*,' he insisted. 'Oh, you're not the only one at fault. It's everywhere. You think, what a magnificent view, get to the door to find the bedroom is overlooking anything but the view!'

I know. It was the bane of my life at times. *That* view! Everyone wants a room with *that* view, though never before were we told we should have ensured a building with all rooms looking out front. Today's grand designs may well measure up to his ideals though not in this part of the world. A square box with tiny windows is the pre-ferred option of our local Planning Authority despite the panoramic views calling out for picture windows. Thankfully, when we built The Sheiling over 40 years ago, Planning was keen to be of assistance, happy to see new houses built in this remote area desperate to retain its population. Today we would not even be allowed the delights of an open fire to while away the cold winter evenings. The vagaries of a planning application, in Sutherland anyway, are designed to send you scurrying elsewhere to build a home. Australia, maybe? With all windows overlooking a view! I should know. Planning our next home, for our retirement remember, it took us near a year to get the building warrant through, and that after the stressful time getting outline planning permission, never mind what was to follow. I wonder if they're any quicker in Australia.

Conscious of the fact everyone wants a view of the bay, we made sure the patios in the back garden had plenty of colour and set up bird feeding stations so there was the additional interest of watching a variety of delightful small birds as they flitted about the garden. We boasted of their tuneful morning chorus, their happy camaraderie as they fluttered round the nut cages and seed dispensers, queuing at the bird-bath, ever so politely, until provocation, bad manners and hideous morning calls took over when invaded by a sudden influx of collar doves.

I had taken the cats aside, when quite young, lecturing them on the niceties of being part of an establishment that could not allow its residents, either four or two legged, to act as they would often wish, in the interests of maintaining good relationships with the paying guests. I emphasised the word *paying*. Murdering these charming little flying machines in full view of bedroom windows was a hanging offence, tradition coupled with temptation being no defence. Perseverance saw to it that birds were no longer stalked in the garden area, difficult though this was when the blackbirds cottoned on and became gung-ho, taking to swanking past the cats, who sit watching with shoulders hunched, tails twitching, ears pinned back but, instead of pouncing, would look furtively behind, checking to see if there happened to be a witness about. Occasionally we found a feather or two, but never saw the deed done, nor did we get complaints from guests.

Until one fine day a couple came in, deeply offended. 'One of your cats killed a bird! I thought it was a bit naïve of you to think cats don't kill birds!'

'That's not like them! Honestly! Our cats don't kill birds. Which cat was it?' I added in contradiction, merely adding to her suspicions that I had lured them into a room to enjoy the birds, to watch in horror as the little darlings were massacred.

'We don't know which of your creatures killed the bird. Feathers! That's all that is left.' Funny. Previous, well remonstrated with 'accidental' kills left wings, legs, beaks, all evidence of the dastardly deed, the cat feverishly promising it would never accidentally bump into a bird again, those birds so nervous they died of fright – and no point wasting good food!

'Was it a collar dove?' I queried, spirits rising. Maybe I still had control of the cats. I had not thought to teach them to brush up the evidence after a supper of collar dove. Trying to teach the cats to distinguish between the acceptable robins, blackbirds, thrush, wrens, chaffinches, siskins, and to encourage breakfasting on collar doves was a feat I studiously attempted to master. The doves were copious to the point of constant annoyance. Their early, very early, calling was enough to waken the dead. Then the starlings arrived, blackening the sky, swirling and swarming and eating everything in sight. The doves were sweetness and light by comparison to those speckled demons of the sky that departed as swiftly as they came, but ever since, a scout or two will arrive, check out to see if there is a large cake for dinner, and within minutes, there are thousands of starlings, possibly millions, keeping all other birds at bay.

My bird-loving couple had forgiven me sufficiently for my cat's ulterior behaviour to join us in a glass of wine the night the feather-leaving culprit was found out. Enjoying the company, sheer relaxation, looking out on the patios from the picture window in our private sitting-room, sun dappling through the trees, birds entertaining as ever, cats well out of the picture, a flash of wings swooped in, zipped through the trees, picking up a song-bird en route. A sparrow-hawk landed, glowering all around, before immediately plucking his catch, leaving the feathers in a little heap then taking to the air again.

My guests' reaction to that! No 'we're so sorry pussy-cats for blaming you'. No offers of 'weren't we silly thinking it naïve you are trained not to catch the song-birds'! Instead, 'Aren't those hawks skilled. Wasn't that magnificent. What other bird could swoop so accurately through trees and pick up its prey.'

Well, that was the shine off the evening for me, but they didn't seem to notice. For some time to come, newly arriving visitors could easily find me prancing about the back green shouting obscenities to the sky, brandishing the long window brush in excited gesticulation, as I rushed to the defence of the small birds each time the hawk swooped by the trees. Part of the car park looked onto this area and could be the reason why a quick glance behind caught sight of cars accelerating back down our driveway. Those who were booked had to be persuaded into the house and gently assured I really was quite sane and all would be well. Trust me. I'm a B&B wifie!

We grew very fond of the birds and got to know the families of blackbirds hatched in the surrounding bushes and trees, the ones who cocked a snoop at the cats who sat there, twitching their tails while the blackbirds sauntered past doing their slow walk without turning a feather. Guests found this highly amusing. The cats did not, and to this day, birds walk and flit about the garden unmolested while three cats go about their business, eyes averted elsewhere. The hawk continues to visit, occasionally, when he thinks the prancing woman with the stick is occupied elsewhere. We find the evidence, delighted this clever bird has sussed out the value of a fat, rather slow, dove above the skimpier meal of song-bird, so my mad forays with the window brush no longer scare off potential visitors.

As to the view, I have learned to tell people, 'I have a double available, overlooking the garden,' whether a view is asked for or not. 'There are some lovely birds you can watch from your window,' as I told another couple who were delighted, their trip being purely to visit the nearby very popular RSPB reserve at Forsinard.

They were charmed by our garden birds and particularly fond of the blackbirds, intrigued by their attitude to the cats, but the day before leaving Mrs Stephens came scurrying into the lounge, highly indignant. 'Do you realise, half those blackbirds out there are starlings!'

Yes, well, that was a problem we had to put up with over the years.

I risked my reputation by being seen in the supermarkets buying at least half a dozen loaves of the cheapest bread I could find, added to which several massive slabs of pure lard did nothing to enhance the image of my cuisine!

Feeble pronouncements of, 'it's for the birds,' at the checkout just got me funny looks but home I came, several times a year, to melt down the lard, make heaps of breadcrumbs – as well as an indescribable mess. I added mounds of bird seed, fruit and nuts, especially peanuts, producing bird cakes that delighted our garden residents but attracted starlings. The starlings never stayed. As soon as the cake was finished, which was not long, off they would swarm. At first I pled in their defence, 'they must eat too,' while they chorused in the background, 'let us eat cake!' But, with their constant loud squabbling, long sharp beaks, bullying our lovely well behaved garden birds, wings wildly fluttering, the area reverberating with their loud quarrelsome squawks, I began to greet their noisy arrivals with a race out to rescue the cake until they were gone. 'Our' birds would then share what was on offer, very peaceably, until the starlings sent out their scouts again and in short order, back they'd all flock, and out I would race, as if I didn't have another thing to do in the world.

One day it dawned on me the bread-maker could do double service and loaves for the birds could be rustled up, saving the embarrassment of buying cheap rubbish and bumping into colleagues whose eyes flit over the contents of your trolley then avert in total horror when they see your purchases. I always feel I make matters worse when I tried to explain. Anyway, into the mix went a mound of bird seed, some nuts and raisins. They scoffed it with complete relish. You've probably guessed the sad end to this tale. I often put good nutty bread with interesting seeds out for the guests, and also there's a particular loaf our oversees visitors love, rich with raisins which goes out now and then.

I have to admit that in the struggle with BT my mind, probably, was not on the job. BT is as handy as any to blame when it came to clearing the table and I took better heed of the last slice of brown bread left on the plate.

'That was absolutely delicious,' a guest smiled, leaving the dining room and if they'd left it at that I would have been less shocked at my carelessness when setting the table. How could I have mixed up the breads? I really was getting too old for the job I decided just as my happy visitor added, 'You must tell me where to get that bread. It's got a most unusual taste and you don't often get the raisins with the seeds and nuts, but we did enjoy it.'

'Oh, that was the last of it, I'm afraid and it's home-made. I often make interesting brown breads,' I added, that being the truth as many of my efforts were too heavy and ended up with the birds, rather than the bird's bread ending up with the guests. I was going to have to keep a better eye on myself and how Skimbleshanks never noticed, I don't know. My guest wandered off perfectly happy and I never said a dicky-bird about it to anyone, until now. So if any of you really, really, enjoyed unusual bread at The Sheiling, just go out and buy a bag of bird seed, a variety of chopped nuts, desiccated coconut and some raisins to chuck into a normal wholemeal mix, and there you have it!

I look at those birds flitting back and fore as I wonder what life will hold, now that I'm about to be free. But free from what? Am I free from the cancer that found its way into the lymph system to nag at the euphoria of a perceived survival? Free soon of the anxiety of keeping up standards, even though I know that all is well, exceeding that well-lauded expectation when I had the confidence to accept a five star rating with its constant challenge of keeping up what was, by comparison, so easy to achieve. Pinning your colours to the highest masthead in the hospitality industry ensures dedicated vigilance and the propensity to attract a certain type of customer, who thrives on wall-to-wall attention and genuinely believes that the entire household should revolve round their needs. That guest, my customer, expects to be my top priority from the moment he or she makes that tentative first enquiry. The freedom to laugh at the sheer audacity of it all will soon be mine.

But with that freedom will come a great loss. We will miss people. That's right, people, the human population who caused us at times to wonder why we did this job. So few caused distress out of the vast majority who stepped over our door, bringing into our world their warm, kind and generous natures, giving friendships that have grown over the years. Some will be back, and others, no matter how well we got on, I know we shall never see again. It is the way of things. And then, there's that other concern. People who stay, even for one night, seem to remember us so well, but I have tremendous trouble in recognising them. Should they happen to visit us when in the area, I will be hard pressed to work out who they are.

I know this because it's happened so often before. When dinner became a thing of the past and determined-to-eat-on-the-premises guests took their custom elsewhere, there I would be, spinning about, making tea and cakes for arrivals. When the doorbell rings, I rush to answer, pleased the expected arrivals have come in time to share tea with whoever else is settling in.

'Hello!' I beam as I open the door expectantly.

'Hello!' they beam back, just as expectantly.

'It's the MacKenzie's!' I offer, all smiles.

Blank stare. 'Isn't it?' I hedge my bets, raising my brows, just in case it is not, which is as well.

'No!' they raise brows back, slightly nonplussed. 'Don't you remember us?' and my stomach starts to lurch. Is it me, or they who have made some kind of error because my last room was booked by MacKenzies who, obviously, they are not. But they are fully expecting my hospitality.

'We stayed with you one night four years ago, when you did dinners. But sadly you don't do that now so we've got in somewhere else and called to see you!' The reason I stopped my Taste of Scotland Dinners was because I was distracted by contracting cancer, which was very inconsiderate of me, I know.

'Oh!' My smile fades a bit.

And in they come, to join the others round the tea table, highly delighted with themselves. Because they have come to see me, I cannot do my usual routine of showing the facilities, providing the tea and an introductory chat, then leaving them to the peace of relaxation with other guests or by themselves. I must stay put, pour myself a cup of whatever and act mine host to people who should be getting their hosting done elsewhere! Much of their conversation bemoans the fact dinner is no longer provided, whipping up mutiny with guests who were never promised dinner. Dinner had not been advertised for some years. Now my dinners were being talked up to as high a standard as Gordon Ramsay would be proud to produce, while under my breath, I produced a considerable number of his best oaths. My own guests then began to feel hard done by, not being offered this largesse from the past. Something was now missing from what hitherto had appeared so perfect an experience.

Or, to get away from such mouth-watering reminiscences, these unexpected visitors spout anecdotal tales to guests who have yet to know the pleasures of this establishment in which they sit open mouthed and showing signs of flight. As they listen to tales from the past, I often see doubt flicker across frozen faces, reflecting back on which so-called friend had lured them to this dubious place to spend part of their precious holiday.

I recall one such incident starting with the innocent question, 'Do you remember when we stayed? Remember, that dog of yours, the one that barked all night, and then in the morning bit that big German lad?'

'What dog? When did that happen?' I say, startled because I did have a dog in the very distant past, my terrier, Roxy, but never did he bite anyone, leave alone a valuable guest. Had it been the cat Smudge, well she was capable of anything, but not barking. Not to my knowledge, though she did believe she was a dog and behaved likewise on many occasions.

'It happened the night we stayed, a few years ago.'

'I don't have a dog,' I anxiously assured my new guests who were sitting up considerably straighter, mouths open, but ever so quiet. 'And I never had one since at least 20 years!'

'Yes, you did. We remember it well, don't we dear?'

'A rabbit. I had a house rabbit, but he didn't bark all night, though he did bite if you really annoyed him.' No. Not him then.

Other detrimental memories from the past, which were no part of my reminiscences, coloured the conversations when visited by people who, at times I thought, must have stayed with someone else. On such an occasion, only last year, a couple who actually came to stay, announced they had stayed with me before, indeed, a very long time ago. Did I not remember them? No, I didn't, no matter how hard I tried.

'My, you've changed a lot,' they greeted me. Yes indeed I have. Gone are the long dark auburn tresses, replaced with a short cut, lightened considerably, courtesy of a small plastic bottle and a good hairdresser. I wasn't going to depart this earth without finding out if blondes had more fun, but I did leave it rather late.

'You've lost such a lot of weight.'

'No, I've always been this size,' slim, I called it, skinny my family insisted, but a fairly steady size ten.

'Oh, we remember you as being... well, more like my wife,' he said without blinking, pointing to his good lady, remonstrating with me that not only had I lost a few stone in weight, but apparently put on a few inches in height. 'Were you always that tall?' he puzzled, continuing before I could butt in. 'You and my wife here were very alike. I remember that well.' By now he was sounding quite hurt as I looked down on his rotund, five foot wife from my near five foot eight inches, none of which were added since I first ventured into B&B.

She did rather resemble a ball. She had a round face, jowls quivering as she nodded in agreement with her husband, small round eyes piercing and mouth grim, eyeing me up and down in an accusing manner, changing like that on them. I was beginning to feel quite guilty until, at last, memory returned when they saw the rest of the house, admitting they had stayed elsewhere where the hostess had indeed fitted a different bill.

So, if past guests who made fleeting stays do come to visit, I'm sure they will forgive the lack of synchronistic recall. At least I will be free from the tender mercies of BT, though whatever they do to me in the future will not have the same devastating effect as on some of my friends whose businesses rely on BT accounts. They relay tales of distress, sometimes through the press, other times as deplorable things happen and they seek a shoulder to cry on. Did I go to litigation? No. I didn't have the time or the energy and that is what BT must rely upon. They wore me down with the difficulty of getting someone to speak to who did not, the instant they heard it was a broadband problem, hoist you off to the Indian call centre to trade your precious time for their inability to pick up quickly on the problem and do something helpful about it.

After reinstatement of my account, it continued to be impossible to get anyone at BT to explain why this had happened and what did *they* think should be compensation for such a drop in business and reputation. Other than the acknowledgement letter, remember, delivery paid for by myself, no reply ever came from dear Sir Christopher Bland, their eminent Chairman. I could send him a copy of this book, postage to be paid by the recipient. A kind gesture considering what they put me through, their final episode defying belief!

Out of the blue one morning came a telephone call from a BT office. It was an English-speaking woman, clear as a bell and nice as nine-pence. This woman was so convincing in her assurance that I would not only get the long-awaited explanation in writing, but she would see to it that I got their legal team's contact details if I did not want to accept the £100 compensation (which BT allowed only if the complaint did not go to litigation) that being all they would offer, and yes, this would be made to me in writing. A paltry sum which in no way defrayed my losses, but knowing my time limits and tendency to put the past behind me when all things bright and beautiful were restored to my life, I agreed to them going ahead with the letter of offer which I was assured would arrive shortly.

This charming woman was adamant when I voiced scepticism that this letter just may not come. She would see to it herself. She had been studying my file, the seriousness of my complaints, including the inconvenience of losing my email account when I was at a crucial stage in publishing *The Land Beyond The Green Fields*, she agreed was not an acceptable situation.

At last I was talking to someone who understood everything, and better still, was in a position to do something effective about it.

Then, to my complete astonishment, she went into an excited explanation of how her young son was an outstanding footballer and had been chosen for one of the Football Academies and she had written this manuscript of how she, as a single parent, was encouraging him. Could I give her any hint as to how to get a publisher!

No, I most decidedly could not. I gave her the advice most publishers gave me. Buy yourself a copy of the Writers' and Artists' Yearbook and get on with it. But, knowing she was my lifeline to satisfaction with BT, I listened for an age. Making knowledgeable murmurs, I wished her all the very best with her book and looked forward to the forthcoming communication that would allow me to choose between accepting their idea of compensation, or taking the advice given by the Federation of Small Business, and take what they believed could be an excellent case to law.

I never got the letter. I never went to law. I had far too many exciting things happen in my life, not to mention the unexpected invitation from VisitScotland to attend their gala night dinner, The Thistle Awards, in Edinburgh. That ended for me in the stunning realisation that it was to be me, the first ever woman and the first person to bring back to the Highlands, that most coveted and highest accolade in the Scottish Tourism calendar, the Scottish Silver Thistle. Awarded, it says on the plaque, for outstanding achievement. That kept my head in a whirl for at least a month.

There was no time to sour the air with chasing after the elusive BT.

There was also the work involved in closing down the business after a quiet autumn. The quietness was fully expected after BT's scuppering of forward bookings. I would never know how many because they lost, into cyberspace, all the backlog of emails stacked up in the weeks awaiting the reinstatement of my account.

The lack of business, despite its accompanying lack of funds, suited me as so much was happening on the tourism front. The newly emerging North Highlands Tourism, a branch of the Prince Charles' Initiative for our three northern counties was emerging as the best opportunity the North has ever had to market to the world such a fascinating geographical spread of land, where visitors would flock if only they knew it existed. To add to that, the Highlands & Islands Tourism Awards were heading for their third and increasingly successful

Gala Event that November after an extremely busy year. There were also highly interesting trips with the Federation of Small Businesses to Bute House, our seat of government in London, and to our Parliament in the Capital City of Edinburgh, one of my favourite places in the whole wide world. No, not Parliament. Edinburgh, of course. I love it. Especially the Royal Mile, where I walk so happily, from the shocking modernity of the Parliament building, hideous to view but good to be inside, way up that fascinating old street to near the Castle where, in the heights of an alluring building, as old as the Castle itself, down a short cobbled wynd, sits the offices of the publishers of my first book on tourism, *Heads on Pillows*.

It was there I sat, with heart in mouth, wondering if I could convince them that the tourism industry, and especially the bed and breakfast sector, was worthy of committing to paper. That risking their reputation and finances on a story that would remind many of the hardships, others of the petty jealousies, so many of the fun, the vast majority of the warmth and comfort to be found at a fraction of the cost of expensive hotel accommodation was wise. The story of those ubiquitous dwellings in the far off days when every community sported at least half a dozen homes willing to take in summer guests.

There are now fewer and fewer bed and breakfasts coming on stream, the way they originated long ago, built from the heart of a home, willing to share its roof with strangers. Many new B&Bs offer the best of accommodation, units built specially in the garden allowing access to the house only at specified times, or wonderfully prestigious houses offering much more than a mere bed for the night accompanied by good food. It is no longer B&B as I knew it, yet I am as guilty as any of being at the forefront of change, a change we believed the visitor wanted. Much of the 'couthiness' is gone, overtaken by efficiency and facilities, driven, as we firmly believed, by the needs of the customer. Attitudes had to change, but whose, I often wondered.

Well, we can wonder as much as we like, so long as we believe: the customer is always right!

Epilogue

I AM VERY AWARE that since writing this book in 2007 time has moved on and changes have come about in the tourism industry that are not reflected in these pages. To do so would have made it impossible to relate stories as they actually happened at the time. And of course, in looking back one has to regale the reader with circumstances that brought about situations unbiased by the fact that things are different now.

When I wrote about the lack of horse riding opportunities, there were very few then that had good hacking rather than pony trekking. Now there are many more businesses in nearly every area of Scotland allowing various ways to holiday with an equine theme.

And then there is the 'going green' aspect. Since first mooted by conscientious operators, backed by the government and tourism agencies with the Green Tourism Business Scheme, this responsible attitude to our future has been adopted by most of the industry. VisitScotland is looking at incorporating recognition of having solid green credentials in its basic marketing costs, ridding the proprietor of the concern, 'can we afford to join their green scheme?' Now that technology has ensured we are much better informed about the value of being green, it would be highly irresponsible not to contribute to the sustainability of our environment. Only this morning a report on the likelihood of more flooding in coming years ended with, 'Attitudes will have to change!' The tourism industry can be proud to be one of the first to have made that change.

The Pride & Passion movement has faded into the ether after some sterling work. However, we now have Tourism Intelligence Scotland. It is not often a project gets the undisputed support of the industry but TIS has proven itself indispensable through a solid and reliable build of tools and information invaluable to the industry. TIS is also behind the production of a series of excellent brochures promoting all that makes Scotland a country not to be missed when scheduling that all-important holiday.

Initiated in Scotland and the envy of many other countries, VisitScotland's quality star rated scheme continues to be rolled out across the world. Yet at home the industry continues to debate its value. How can this be when the level of customer complaints has dropped year-on-year for businesses in the QA scheme, while complaints against businesses outside the scheme continue to rise.

In recent years, VisitScotland has been revamped to have a stronger relationship with businesses, determined to engage at all levels with the people who are responsible for the welfare of our visitors. Time will tell how well this re-assessment of positions and policies works. Our Inspectors of old are now Quality Tourism Advisors, engaging in a much more business-like manner.

The re-launch in April of VisitScotland's new national consumer website, now poised to make a major contribution to how the world sees this undeniably fascinating small country, has already seen a huge increase in traffic to its site. I can no longer look at this site from an operator's point of view, but as a consumer, well done VisitScotland. I like it and so do many others!

As ever, it is up to the businesses themselves to take advantage of prime marketing opportunities like this. But the fear is forever present that with more and more funding ploughed into delivering such large projects, will the cost of belonging drive out small operators running bed and breakfast and self-catering establishments.

But the biggest change of all comes courtesy of the internet. Businesses are more in control of their marketing opportunities through building inspirational new websites and choosing their own vehicles to get their message out across the world-wide-web. Those who promise more than they deliver had better watch out. The internet can turn round and bite you. The advent of online reviews through Tripadvisor has grown to be the bible of the consumer, serving the travelling public as an indicator as to what to really expect from the establishment – after you've had a look at what is offered through its own website. Some reviews have to be taken with a pinch of salt, but generally speaking, it's a good indication of what is really in store.

Remember the Taste of Scotland food accreditation scheme? It's some years since it passed into oblivion despite its highly rated appreciation by both consumer and operator alike. Now our food grading scheme is Eatscotland and the cry goes out, bring back the Taste of Scotland. There are great quality places to eat and drink throughout Scotland and we have lots of companies to promote our fresh produce worthy of a country that boasts some of the finest fresh foods in the world. It's getting that information out to our customer that is key to maintaining the establishments that live up to that proud boast.

And finally, what about our bed and breakfasts? How are they actually doing as the customer gets ever more discerning and the product gets ever more expensive to deliver? I heralded the demise of the sector long ago, and not due to the growing needs of today's traveller, or the disappearance of enterprise grants, or the prohibitive cost of setting up a new B&B. For me the writing was on the wall listening to young people talk, watching their life-style and expectations as they set up homes. They gave no indication they ever wanted to share that home with strangers. And can you see today's young couples giving up the social activities that govern much of their lives? It's a big ask, and I see only those who have moved past these early exciting years give consideration to offering bed and breakfast in their homes as a means to support their life styles. Today the early morning news bulletin highlighted more and more bed and breakfast premises coming onto the market with few selling, yet tourism is surviving the pangs of the recession better than many other sectors.

In this year of Creative Scotland 2012 my wish is that people with the necessary entrepreneurial spirit will be inspired to create many more ways to offer welcoming beds in their homes, offering food and facilities they can be proud of as they support a sector of the tourism industry that is quintessentially Scottish, based on hospitality that is as old as the hills. And may this hospitality continue to be with us as long as the hills remain.

Joan Campbell
Stoneybraes
12 July 2012

Heads on Pillows: Behind the Scenes at a Highland B&B

Joan Campbell
ISBN 978-1-906307-71-4 PBK £9.99

With so many people looking to leave the rat-race and start their own bed and breakfast in the country, *Heads on Pillows* give readers a personal glimpse into the unique world of B&Bs, where owners open up their own homes for guests to enjoy.

This book offers witty anecdotes, personal experiences and helpful hints to anyone who aspires to enter the trade, from an award-winning B&B owner. From its modest beginnings as a single room B&B to the first five star Bed and Breakfast in the northern counties of Scotland, follow the story of the Sheiling and its owner.

Part autobiography and part 'how to' guide, *Heads on Pillows* is both informative and entertaining.
This true account charts the growth and the development of the Scottish tourist trade, especially in the Highlands where the Sheiling is located, and offers through the experience of over 30 years an unparalleled insight into the Bed and Breakfast trade that is so enticing to so many.

Foreword by Peter Lederer, Chairman of VisitScotland and managing director of the famous Gleneagles hotel.

With a witty, informative and enjoyable narrative, the book recounts the trials and tribulations of working in the tourist industry.
CAITHNESS COURIER

The book is a great anecdotal collection of stories that peek behind the smiling facade of the woman running the best B&B in the North.
LESLEY RIDDOCH

The Northern Highlands: The Empty Lands

Tom Atkinson

ISBN 978-1-842820-87-2 PBK £6.99

The Empty Lands are that great area of northern Scotland between Ullapool and Cape Wrath, and between Bonar Bridge and John O' Groats. It is truly the Land of the Mountain and the Flood, where land and sea mingle in unsurpassed glory. From the pier-head at Ullapool to the Smoo Caves at Durness, and from Dornoch Cathedral to Dounreay Nuclear Establishment, Tom Atkinson describes it all, with his usual deep love for the land and its people. Myths and legends, history, poetry, and a keen eye for the landscape and all its creatures make this book an essential companion for all who travel to that magnificent part of Scotland.

The essence of Scotland's far north and west is emptiness. Emptiness of people, that is, but of nothing else that brings delight to any tired soul, writes Atkinson, I have tried to convey something of the sheer magic of the Highlands, something of the joy that comes from such a cornucopia of loveliness, for the Highlands are lovely beyond words.

Scots We Ken

Julie Davidson

ISBN 978-1-906307-00-4 HBK £9.99

'We dinny do bairns in this pub. We dinny do food, apart from peanuts and crisps, or music or fruit machines or video games. We jist aboot do television, but thon set on the wall is 20 years old and it only gets turned on fur internationals or Scotsport. This pub is fur drinkin.'

From 'The Last Publican'

Natives know them. Visitors soon get to know them. Some, like the Golf Club Captain, the Last Publican and the Nippy

Sweetie, are an endangered species; others, like the Whisky Bore and the Munrobagger, are enduring figures on the Scottish landscape. Every generation produces its own variations on the Scottish character and it doesn't take long for the newcomers to become familiar social types like the MSP, the Yooni Yah, the Country Commuter and the Celebrity Chieftain. Most Scots, if they're honest, will recognise a little bit of themselves in one or other of these mischievous and frighteningly accurate portraits.

A triumph of canny Scots-watching.
MURRAY GRIGOR

Riddoch on the Outer Hebrides

Lesley Riddoch

ISBN 978-1-906307-86-8 PBK £12.99

Riddoch on the Outer Hebrides is a thought-provoking commentary based on broadcaster Lesley Riddoch's cycle journey through a beautiful island chain facing seismic cultural and economic change. Her experience is described in a typically affectionate but hard-hitting style; with humour, anecdote and a growing sympathy for islanders tired of living at the margins but wary of closer contact with mainland Scotland.

Let's be proud of standing on the outer edge of a crazy mainstream world – when the centre collapses, the periphery becomes central.
ALISTAIR MCINTOSH

She has a way of shining the magnifying glass on a well-documented place in a new and exciting way matching every beauty with a cultural wart that builds to create one of the most unfalteringly real images of the islands – all the more astounding for coming from an outsider.
STORNOWAY GAZETTE

Women of the Highlands

Katharine Stewart

ISBN 978-1-906817-92-3 PBK £7.99

The Highlands of Scotland are an evocative and mysterious land, cut off from the rest of Scotland by mountains and developing as a separate country for hundreds of years. Epitomising the 'sublime' in philosophical thought of the eighteenth century, the Highlands have been a source of inspiration for poets and writers of all descriptions.

Katharine Stewart takes us to the heart of the Highlands with this history of the women who shaped this land. From the women of the shielings to the Duchess of Gordon, from bards to conservationists, authors to folk-singers, *Women of the Highlands* examines how the culture of the Highlands was created and passed down through the centuries, and what is being done to preserve it today.

Details of these and other books published by Luath Press can be found at:
www.luath.co.uk

Luath Press Limited

committed to publishing well written books worth reading

LUATH PRESS takes its name from Robert Burns, whose little collie Luath (*Gael.*, swift or nimble) tripped up Jean Armour at a wedding and gave him the chance to speak to the woman who was to be his wife and the abiding love of his life. Burns called one of 'The Twa Dogs' Luath after Cuchullin's hunting dog in Ossian's *Fingal*. Luath Press was established in 1981 in the heart of Burns country, and is now based a few steps up the road from Burns' first lodgings on Edinburgh's Royal Mile.
Luath offers you distinctive writing with a hint of unexpected pleasures.

Most bookshops in the UK, the US, Canada, Australia, New Zealand and parts of Europe either carry our books in stock or can order them for you. To order direct from us, please send a £sterling cheque, postal order, international money order or your credit card details (number, address of cardholder and expiry date) to us at the address below. Please add post and packing as follows: UK – £1.00 per delivery address; overseas surface mail – £2.50 per delivery address; overseas airmail – £3.50 for the first book to each delivery address, plus £1.00 for each additional book by airmail to the same address. If your order is a gift, we will happily enclose your card or message at no extra charge.

ILLUSTRATION: IAN KELLAS

Luath Press Limited

543/2 Castlehill
The Royal Mile
Edinburgh EH1 2ND
Scotland

Telephone: 0131 225 4326 (24 hours)
Fax: 0131 225 4324
email: sales@luath.co.uk
Website: www.luath.co.uk